Fulfill Your Dreams

Endorsements

In his new book *Fulfill Your Dreams: Seize the Day and Be Extraordinary*, Dr. Bob Sawvelle has not only captured the very heart of what Jesus provides for every believer, for us to both understand and embrace, but with thoughtful and practical biblical explanation, Bob invites us to lay hold of the truth about our Christ-given identity and glorious future as sons and daughters of God. As a reader, we are encouraged to dream with God, begin a daily practice of renewing our mindset through prayer and application, and lead a lifestyle of forgiveness. Bob writes an eye-opening perspective on the importance of faith and laying hold of the increase we have available in Christ.

Fulfill Your Dreams: Seize the Day and Be Extraordinary presents the way to step forward and truly embrace your Kingdom destiny. I believe this book tackles the very real stronghold of a lack of personal faith facing the church today on most every continent where I have had the privilege of ministering. Throughout his writing Bob teaches that the power of the Kingdom lies in the development of intimacy with God, the practice of renewing our minds and stepping out in faith to do what Jesus said we would do in Matthew 10:7-8. As we read and engage, we cannot help but be encouraged to act upon the truth that we are the passionate ones spoken of in Matthew 11:12: *"From the moment John the Baptist stepped onto the scene until now, the realm of heaven's kingdom is bursting forth and passionate people have taken hold of its power."*

Rev. Joanne Moody
Agape Freedom Fighters
Sacramento, CA

Dr. Bob Sawvelle lives what he preaches. Bob's preparation and journey in Christ has taken him to a place where he is fulfilling God's call and destiny for his life. In his book, *Fulfill Your Dreams: Seize the Day and Be Extraordinary*, Bob shares biblical principles to help you fulfill the purpose for which God has created you. Bob shares some of his spiritual journey, along with relevant stories of others, to build upon the biblical teaching themes in the book.

Fulfill Your Dreams: Seize the Day and Be Extraordinary will help you discover the amazing plan God has for your life and provide you with practical tools to assist you in fulfilling that plan. God is ordering your steps, so seize the day and fulfill your dreams!

Dr. Nick Gough
Senior Pastor, Faith Center
Great Falls, MT

Bob Sawvelle is not taking us on an abstract journey. This book has shoe leather. It was pounded out in the life of a man who did just what he is asking us to do. *Fulfill Your Dreams: Seize the Day and Be Extraordinary* is inspirational, informative and practical. Within this book is the wisdom of a sage, the heart of a child, and the adventure of a pioneer. He writes to invite us into our own encounter with the One who alone can fill us with his dreams and make them our reality. Read and be changed.

Dr. Alan Hawkins
Senior Pastor, New Life City Church
Albuquerque, NM

Fulfill Your Dreams

SEIZE THE DAY AND BE EXTRAORDINARY

—ɯ—

Principles to help you fulfill dreams by embracing the
purpose for which God has created you

Bob Sawvelle

Fulfill Your Dreams
Seize the Day and Be Extraordinary

Bob Sawvelle
info@passiontucson.org
passiontucson.org
bobsawvelle.com

ISBN-13: 978-1725814295
ISBN-10: 1725814293

Passion Church
1212 South Palo Verde Ave.
Tucson, AZ 85713

Library of Congress Cataloging-in-Publication Data (Pending)

Dedication

To Carolyn, who has journeyed tirelessly with me to fulfill God's purpose for our lives. Your willingness to live a life of adventurous faith has encouraged me, often when I needed it most. You chose to follow Jesus' call on our lives, no matter how risky, over security and comfort. You are an example of one who has seized the day and lived an extraordinary life, that others might know him.

Table of Contents

Foreword

—⁓—

BOB SAWVELLE'S *FULFILL YOUR DREAMS: Seize the Day and Be Extraordinary* is an amazing book about living victoriously. Dr. Sawvelle draws upon the Bible, his personal experiences, history, and contemporary stories to make the book enjoyable to read. Each chapter opens to the reader great insight into the tools needed to live a more abundant life.

Beginning with the understanding that God made each of us extraordinary, Bob develops the importance of not allowing your failures to define you. Only you can live your journey and understand the reality of our new life in Christ—that we are a new person, with a new mind, new life, new freedom, and new authority—that opens higher realms of dreaming with God. Bob also discusses some of the potential pitfalls along the journey, including how to rid ourselves of a slave mentality, live in forgiveness, and embrace a worry-free mindset. Through our relationship with Christ, practicing faith-filled prayer and understanding our position in God, we can partner with God in fulfilling the dreams he places in our hearts.

Overall, I found the book most practical, biblical, informative, and faith-building. It would be beneficial for anyone who wants to live an extraordinary life and fulfill not only their own dreams but discover God's greater dream for their life.

Dr. Randy Clark
Founder of Global Awakening and Overseer of the Apostolic Network of Global Awakening
Mechanicsburg, PA

Introduction

—⚞⚟—

FOLLOWING JESUS IS THE GREATEST joy for the believer. Each day offers new possibilities. Every challenge is an opportunity to overcome and achieve the impossible. Setback and failure provide back doors to success. Every accomplishment and goal achieved builds confidence to overcome and succeed in life. Fulfilled dreams are the result of consistent achievements through the hardships of life. With God, all things are possible.

The book of Ephesians is inspiring. According to Paul, living in God's realm is normal for the follower of Christ: "Glory to God, who is able to do far beyond all that we could ask or imagine by his power at work within us" (Eph. 3:20 CEB). This passage challenges us to live beyond ourselves and to trust Jesus for his empowering grace to face every challenge optimistically.

The Apostle Paul's letter to the Ephesian church is a high watermark for his writings. Paul's writing displays a profoundly mystical element and he offers a transcendent and glorious view of Jesus, the church, and the believer. For Paul, the follower of Christ lives in spiritual union with the victorious resurrection life of the Son of God, which spiritually elevates the believer to Christ's heavenly realm and ascended glory. The follower of Jesus lives from his victory toward our earthly realm.

According to Paul, God's power and grace work in the life of a Christian to create the nature of Jesus in one's heart. The Holy Spirit also empowers the believer to live beyond their human abilities. Paul describes the grace of the Holy Spirit's ongoing work in and through a believer—accomplishing more than a person could ever ask for or imagine.

Is it possible that understanding God's power to work in and through a believer could be the key to unlocking a life of unusual activity and creativity? I believe so. God created you to be an extraordinary person. Your life in Christ, empowered by the Spirit, enables you to operate in his revelation and power to accomplish God-inspired dreams and works as you faithfully follow Jesus.

It is my desire for this book to examine how a person can move beyond normalcy to living life extraordinarily—fulfilling ambitions, goals, and dreams. In *Fulfill Your Dreams - Seize the Day and Be Extraordinary*, you will learn how to follow Jesus courageously and partner effectively with him to minister to others and fulfill your created purpose.

I will examine positive principles—learning how to dream God-sized dreams, living from your new identity in Christ, walking in love, becoming a person of faith and courage, and developing a strong prayer life—that empower you to fulfill your destiny. I will also discuss negative mindsets that need to be removed—false identity, unforgiveness, worry, and fear—that can prevent you from fulfilling your dreams and living as God intended.

My intent is to provide you with kingdom principles to live a life of audacious faith, free from the pain of the past and routine of the present, to focus on intimate relationship with Jesus and fulfill the impossible. The following chapters contain principles to aid you in your development and assist you in achieving your goals and destiny. You will read about some of my life lessons and meet a few others who have followed Jesus to find their extraordinary calling.

Are you ready to *fulfill your dreams*? Join me and learn key kingdom principles to live life to the fullest and fulfill your created purpose and destiny.

CHAPTER 1

You're Extraordinary

—ɯɯ—

"I give thanks to you that I was marvelously set apart.
Your works are wonderful—I know that very well."

— PSALM 139:14 CEB

"There are only two ways to live your life. One is as though
nothing is a miracle. The other is as if everything is."

— ALBERT EINSTEIN

WHY BE NORMAL?

HAVE YOU HEARD THE COMMON expression, "Why be normal?" God's original design for each of us was not simply to be "normal." You were created for more than merely existing; God made you in his image to live a life that reflects his glory and divine nature. Your life is nothing short of miraculous.

As part of his divine plan and purpose, God places within each of us a desire to be extraordinary. The Psalmist wrote, "You saw me before I was born. Every day of my life was recorded in your book. Every moment was laid out before a single day had passed" (Psalm 139:16 NLT). None of us, regardless of the circumstances that brought us into this world, are here by accident or chance. No matter who you are and regardless of your past or present circumstances, you were fearfully and wonderfully made to have a life that is meaningful and makes a difference in this world (Psalm 139:14).

Extraordinary is defined as: "1) going beyond what is usual, regular, or customary; 2) exceptional to a very marked extent."[1] Going beyond what is usual. Exceptional. One could even say beyond normal. Indeed, it would seem that asking ourselves, "Why be normal?" is an important question to consider. What may appear abnormal might just be that someone had enough courage to pursue something radical, beyond what is usual. You were created by God to live above mediocrity; you were destined to accomplish important things in this life.

I define normalcy as living the status quo, or below one's potential, while extraordinary is living a life which achieves God's ordained purpose. You were marvelously set apart by God for something special: to find your purpose and pursue it with passion. Your calling is unique to you, and it may or may not look like what the world would value. It may mean living as a successful mother raising godly children, becoming a CEO and influencing many, being a good husband who works a job with excellence for God's honor, or perhaps leaving the security of a career to follow Jesus into the foreign mission field. Your purpose is where you find passion and meaning. Extraordinary living is when we fulfill the calling and assignment God has given us.

SEIZE THE DAY

The Latin phrase *carpe diem*, meaning "seize the day," was popularized after the 1989 movie *Dead Poets Society*. In the film Robin Williams played John Keating, a man who loved poetry and worked as a passionate English teacher at a boy's Ivy League preparatory school. In one of the early scenes, John led his class of young men into the school foyer where several trophy cases lined the walls. In these cases were pictures of previous classes and the trophies they had won. Mr. Keating, or "O' Captain" as some of the boys referred to him, told the boys in dramatic fashion to look closely at some of the old team photos of the young men that preceded them. The youth began to look with awe and wonder as Mr. Keating, like an old sage, declared,

> They're not that different from you, are they? Same hair-cuts. Full of hormones, just like you. Invincible, just like you feel. The world is their oyster. They believe they are destined for great things, just like many of you. Their eyes are full of hope, just like you. Did they wait until it was too late to make from their lives even one iota of what they were capable? Because, you see gentlemen, these boys are now fertilizing daffodils. But if you listen real close, you can hear them whisper their legacy to you. Go on, lean in. Listen, you hear it?—Carpe—hear it?— Carpe, carpe diem. Seize the day boys, make your lives extraordinary![2]

Throughout the movie, this impassioned English teacher strove to impart zeal, creativity, his love of poetry, and a love of life into these boys. Some received freedom from their fears and timid-ity and attempted that which they thought was otherwise impos-sible. Still others brazenly misdirected their zeal and passion toward wrong pursuits. Mr. Keating saw the potential in these boys and dared them to live life to its fullest, and to make their lives matter—to become extraordinary people.

Years ago, this movie deeply impacted me. I thought to myself, "Seize the day—make your lives extraordinary—that's a truth everyone needs to be reminded of daily." Even as I write this, my mind wanders to times when I seized the day and later saw the fruit of my pursuit, even though sometimes years would pass before I fulfilled a goal or realized a dream. Yet, I also remember days and seasons of my life, before I understood some important life principles, when I missed opportunities. There were many times when I found myself hindered by a past event or overcome with feelings of inadequacy.

The truth is that we will all be "fertilizing daffodils" one day. Your ability to overcome your fears, hurts, and the failures of the past will determine the richness of your life today and the legacy you leave for tomorrow. Change and transformation is the path forward for overcomers.

Many people resign themselves to lives of mediocrity rather than embarking on God's process of transformation. Fullness of potential and creativity occur through changes that renew our perspective. God's grace empowers us to be healed and enables progress, but it requires surrendering to the process. So many people are debilitated by the pain of the past; they look within themselves and feel unworthy or unqualified to follow their hopes and dreams to become the people of purpose they were destined to be.

Yet some people seem to be unhindered by the past and courageously move forward, living lives of excellence and achievement, even though of course no one is perfect in their pursuit of fulfillment. In part, their success and courage may be due to their internal makeup, personality type, upbringing or life's circumstances, but these factors are not always the ingredients of real strength and courage. I have observed many who, by all accounts, should have led extraordinary lives but were sadly unable to do so. Still others have had the most challenging circumstances come against them, yet remarkably they have gone on to accomplish noteworthy things and find fulfillment and happiness.

CREATED TO BE EXTRAORDINARY

As you learn how to rely on God's inner strength and resolve, you are positioned to live beyond mediocrity. Jesus, the light of the world (John 8:12), provides revelation, wisdom, faith, and courage to empower you to be extraordinary. When we put our faith in Christ, the believer spiritually unites with Jesus through the indwelling of the Holy Spirit. The Spirit comforts, guides and empowers us to progress into all that God intended us to be—not the least of which is to become like Christ in nature.

This divine union with Jesus is fascinating. The apostle Paul explains, "We are God's masterpiece. He has created us anew in Christ Jesus, so we can do the good things he planned for us long ago" (Eph. 2:10 NLT). You see, you are God's masterpiece, his unique creation destined to accomplish the good things he planned for you long ago. In some respects, you have to try pretty hard *not* to be extraordinary!

When we are genuinely transformed by the love and grace of Christ, he instills with in us new desires for good works and an exceptional life. God cooperates with you in order to accomplish everything he puts on your heart or places before you. He wants you to succeed and make a difference in this world. After all, you are his grand creation, his masterpiece.

This type of life requires humility and a willingness to change. It takes humility to look inside yourself and admit that maybe your life could be more than what you are currently living. Perhaps mindsets or beliefs you hold about yourself empower a lie that hinders you from moving forward in God and in life.

Maybe you have developed a *loser's limp* mentality—an attitude of defeat even before you begin the "game" or attempt to fulfill your dream. A loser's limp occurs when an athlete fakes a limp or injury to mask perceived defeat, and this mentality may present itself as an attitude of, "Why should I even try to do my best? I'm going to lose anyway!" This internal defense mechanism may protect us from disappointment or embarrassment when we fear losing the race or big game, or not getting that job or promotion—or whatever our desire or dream may be—but it is not without cost to extraordinary living.

Our hearts may develop a negative mindset for any number of reasons. For the Christian, it is often linked to a lack of faith and trust in God, which may stem from an area of the mind that is unrenewed and does not fully accept God's truths. We may know the scriptures, but if our heart does not fully believe or understand what Christ has done for us, we may begin to develop a perspective that life is "stacked against us." Bad experiences or circumstances may begin to direct us rather than God's Word and Spirit. If you live from a negative mindset, your life will fall below God's intent, and you may wrongly assume that you cannot achieve an abundant life.

The Holy Spirit loves adventure and a Spirit-filled life of faith is a risky, adventurous one. For you to go to the next level in God—to take another positive step toward the dreams you are longing for—you must cultivate a faith-filled, courageous heart through your dynamic relationship with Christ. Extraordinary living requires great faith and courage. Keep in mind that you are given a measure of faith, but it must be cultivated through reading God's word, obeying it, and allowing the Holy Spirit to lead and guide you through the daily life opportunities that put your faith at risk. It is a faith that sees the invitation of God, understands there will be risks, and is so secure in God's love that our heart shouts, "Yes God, I see the moment. I will seize my day!"

YOUR FAILURES DON'T DEFINE YOU

I will never forget that Saturday morning. Carolyn and I were newly married, and I was in my home office listening to a Christian radio program describing the life of African missionary Dr. David Livingston when God suddenly "called." I was pondering the sacrificial life of Dr. Livingston when I heard the Lord say to me, "I'm calling you into the ministry. Will you serve me wherever I send you?" Tears began to stream down my face as God's presence filled the room.

I responded to God, not irreverently, but from a sincere heart. "Lord, you have the wrong man. You know my failures; I went through a divorce a couple of years ago, how could you ever use me?" I waited for a moment, and heard the Lord answer, "Your failures don't define your calling, but your response to my call determines your destiny." I stood in my office, stunned. I knew this was the Lord speaking to my heart, but my mind was focused on my failures.

My mind needed to be renewed to grasp the truth of my identity in Christ and the reality of God's empowering grace that turns failures into opportunities for success. I've heard it said that "God can win with any hand!" This is true. As Paul explains, "We know that God causes everything to work together for the good of those who love God and are called according to his purpose for them" (Rom. 8:28 NLT). When we are convinced of God's love, acceptance, and goodness toward us, we can then trust him to remake our lives into something glorious.

It would be another couple of years before I firmly believed my identity in Christ and God's call to ministry, despite my failures. Yet as Carolyn and I continued to yield to God's purpose and process, our lives dramatically changed. We began to serve the body of Christ in various capacities, both stateside and overseas. We still had setbacks along the way, but the successes began to outnumber our failures. As we grew in grace, our confidence in God grew as well.

Eventually God led us to sell our business, leave our engineering careers, and follow the Lord full time to reach others with the good news of the kingdom of God. Our faith was stretched and challenged, but as we relied on God, his grace abounded. We began to experience what it meant to live life abundantly; not in earthly riches but in the "righteousness and peace and joy in the Holy Spirit" (Rom. 14:17) which has elevated us and those to whom we have ministered. Today, thirty years later, we are humbled and amazed at how many have been impacted by God's love and power because we said "yes" to God—despite the failures of our past.

In working with people from both the secular and religious realms over the years, I have noticed that the past paralyzes many people. Some freeze because of fear. Others plateau and become comfortable with mediocrity. Yet others successfully move forward to fulfill their desires in life. Not everyone fits neatly into one of these categories, yet here's a thought: what if you were completely free from the pain of past negative life experiences and mindsets, walked fulfilled and empowered today, and carried a hope-filled, expectant view of your future? What if you could seize today's opportunities in such a way that you bring your desired future into existence?

Have you ever failed? This is a rhetorical question; everyone fails at some point along life's journey. It is part of being human. As I wrote earlier, it is the way we handle failure that determines whether we move forward optimistically or remain stuck due to our past.

Jesus specializes in restoring failures and this has been displayed in the lives of so many men and women who were used significantly by God. Consider the Apostle Peter who insisted, "Lord, even if everyone else deserts you, I never will." Jesus replied, "I tell you the truth, Peter—this very night, before the rooster crows twice, you will deny three times that you even know me" (Mark 14:29-30 NLT). That night Peter denied the Lord three times. He failed miserably. After Jesus' resurrection he restored Peter, asking him three times whether he would shepherd God's people. Peter said "yes," and went on to become a leading disciple and eminent apostle who died as a martyr for Jesus. Your failures don't define your destiny, but your response to your past does.

LIVE THE JOURNEY

I love what the writer states in the beginning of Hebrews 12,

> Therefore, since we are surrounded by such a huge crowd of witnesses to the life of faith, let us strip off every weight that slows us down, especially the sin that so easily trips us up. And let us run with endurance the race

God has set before us. We do this by keeping our eyes on
Jesus, the champion who initiates and perfects our faith.
Because of the joy awaiting him, he endured the cross,
disregarding its shame. Now he is seated in the place of
honor beside God's throne. (Heb. 12:1-2 NLT)

There is a race that only you can run, a life that only you can
live. Jesus endured the cross and all of its suffering because of
the joy that awaited him. He knew the intention that the Father
had for humanity: restoration to him in love through giving his
life sacrificially. Believers throughout church history have been
able to live the way Jesus demonstrated, empowered by the Spirit
with a heavenly perspective that seemed abnormal to most. By
keeping their eyes on Jesus, they loved others and endured hardship with an eye on their prize, which is the upward call of God
in Christ. They looked toward a day full of joy in the presence of
God, knowing that it was all worth it so that others might know
this loving savior and friend. The true prize is realized when the
lives of others are impacted through the way we live on this side
of eternity. That is the highest calling of any Christian and the
hallmark of extraordinary living.

Whatever your dreams may be, a life of real success is measured in the way that we love, give, and radiate the very presence
of Jesus—this is our highest calling and the hallmark of extraordinary living. Not everyone is called to full-time Christian ministry or a foreign mission field, but every follower of Jesus is called
to be an ambassador for Christ in whatever capacity or sphere
God places you: family, job, career, etc. As followers of Christ,
we have the privilege of representing him to those around us in
a world that longs to know him. When this becomes your heart-
beat, you are now becoming the person God created you to be.

The book of Proverbs tells us that "When there's no vision, the people get out of control, but whoever obeys instruction is happy" (Prov. 29:18 CEB). God invites us to journey with him, and he reveals his heart and plans to his people (Deut. 29:29). Prophetic vision empowers Christ followers—if you can see what God is offering and attend to it, you not only have the potential to attain it, but will also be empowered by his grace to see it become a reality. The question is: are you willing to catch God's vision for a life of courageous, obedient faith that will empower you to be the person you were created to be? It is worth striving for above everything else. Go after it. Ask God for his dream for your life, and then dare to risk everything to follow Jesus obediently.

Life is not about playing it safe; it is about daily asking God for vision and purpose, to see those in the margins of society and in the world around you. You may be well known, or you may be one of the nameless and faceless people of your generation who is destined to influence many, but never known by the masses. When Jesus becomes the center of your life, it does not matter whether your story is told or you remain hidden; it is important to glorify the King.

Carolyn and I saw the potential of the vision God offered us. Despite our past failures, hardships and setbacks, we attended to the dream Jesus gave us. God transformed and empowered us to pursue his call for our lives, and our lives have been fulfilling as a result. We stopped looking for a life of comfort, and began to live with a courageous faith that was willing to risk. To see God's purpose unfold, we learned obedience to Jesus' leading— no matter how costly. We discovered that comfort and security are often opposed to the radical faith that positions people for extraordinary living.

The journey is part of the destination in life. How are you living your journey? Is your focus on your ambitions and goals, or is your life about following Jesus unreservedly, dreaming with him to see the impossible become probable? As you abandon yourself to God, your dreams will begin to unfold and God's peace will guide you. Choosing to live fully in Christ is the first step to unlocking God's grace through you in fullness of creativity, accomplishments, and realized dreams.

Would you love to have the courage, like Caleb, to "ask for another mountain" each time an opportunity presents itself? How about just facing each day with the hope that comes from serenity and peace of mind, knowing that you can enjoy today without worry of tomorrow? We live in a world of limitless opportunities and I'm just optimistic enough to believe that the impossible can be probable. Through grace, our lives can display exemplary character and works while we also enjoy the journey with God along the way.

My prayer for you is that during this season you will be empowered by God—who is able to do immeasurably more than anything we could ask or imagine, according to his power (Eph. 3:20)—to be a courageous follower of Christ and to be influential in your relationships, families, and however God should lead you. To live today courageously and see tomorrow fulfilled, you must seize today and proactively position yourself in God's revealed will to realize your dreams.

Are you ready to bring your future into reality today? Are you ready to make your life extraordinary, to go to the next level in God that forever changes you? "Go on, lean in. Listen, you hear it?—Carpe—hear it?—Carpe, carpe diem, seize the day boys, make your life extraordinary!"

CHAPTER 2

God-Sized Dreams

—⁓—

"… What kind of dreams have you dreamed?"

— *GENESIS 37:10 CEB*

"The future belongs to those who believe
in the beauty of their dreams."

— *ELEANOR ROOSEVELT*

YOU, TOO, CAN BECOME GREAT…

HANNIBAL, MISSOURI IS THE CHILDHOOD home of Samuel Langhorne Clemens, a man whom most people remember by his pen name, Mark Twain. Later in Twain's life, Hannibal became the setting for two of his most well-known books: *The Adventures of Huckleberry Finn* and *The Adventures of Tom Sawyer.*[1] If you travel to Hannibal today, you will notice the city's attempts to recreate and preserve the feel and genre of what the nineteenth century Midwest Mississippi River culture was like back in Twain's day. A few summers ago, while traveling through the area to a family reunion in the Midwest, my family and I had the opportunity to visit this quaint town.

My favorite site in Hannibal was a large white wooden fence around one of the buildings, erected in honor of a story in Twain's *The Adventures of Tom Sawyer*. Perhaps you recall it: Tom Sawyer convinced some boys to help him paint his Aunt Polly's large fence, which was "thirty yards of board fence nine feet high."[2] If you do the math, you will discover that this is about 800 square feet of fence.

Tom persuaded the boys that painting the fence would be fun, even a privilege. Then he capitalized on this "free" help, taking it easy while they painted the fence. Despite Tom taking advantage of the boys with his bribe of trading trinkets for work, you must give Twain and his character Tom Sawyer an "A" for leadership delegation. Anyone who can convince others to help paint a fence in the Midwest summer heat is either a good sales person or a visionary leader.

I love what Mark Twain said regarding pursuing your dreams: "Keep away from people who try to belittle your ambitions. Small people always do that, but the great make you feel that you, too, can become great." Perhaps Twain was thinking of this quote when he wrote this story. Maybe Tom Sawyer was helping all his friends think and feel like they were on the verge of greatness by painting an old wooden fence on a sweltering summer day. Maybe the subtle implication was, "You too can become another Picasso, and it begins here, gentlemen, with painting this beautiful fence!"

Exceptional people will make you feel like you can excel. Maybe when you were young, a parent, schoolteacher, coach, or pastor told you that you could accomplish remarkable things in life. Perhaps somewhere along the journey, those words have faded, and the reality of making a living, raising a family, and dealing with the complexities and setbacks of life have caused you to doubt that you could fulfill your ambitions and dreams.

Your biggest admirer—your biggest fan—is God himself. He is the loving, nurturing father figure that perhaps you never had, who is beside you to help you "seize the day" and become extraordinary. God invites you into abundant living, where dreams are possible. If you can hear his voice, I believe he is telling you, "Don't give up, it's not too late, only dream big with me!"

GOD HAS YOUR FUTURE IN MIND

I mentioned in chapter one that you are loved and desired by God and that your life has meaning and purpose. To see your dreams fulfilled, you must believe and embrace the truth that the Creator of the universe loves you and has your best interest in mind. He created you in his image and knows your future. Regardless of the poor choices you may have made or negative situations you're faced with, God's love for you is unconditional and complete. He is the most loving, kind, merciful and compassionate being in the universe.

Despite how some people may have portrayed God, he is not angry with you. He is not waiting to execute his judgment on you or on humanity; rather, his "mercy triumphs over judgment." I realize that for some reading this, circumstances and life's events may appear to disprove this, but it is an evil lie that God is angry or perhaps out to "get you." He is not an angry judge waiting to execute his judgment on you or humanity.

The truth is precisely the opposite: God desires to restore you, transform you, and give you hope and a future (Jer. 29:11). In fact, it is this revelation, deep in your heart, of his mercy and goodness that leads you back to him when you have wandered. Yes, you can grieve his Spirit (Eph. 4:30), but God is forgiving and compassionate. He is a Father who loves you, knows you, and cares for you (Psalm 103). He longs to draw you near to himself when you have wandered (Luke 15). His deepest desire for you and for all of humanity is to turn to him (2 Pet. 3:9) and trust him.

Jesus is the full expression of God's love. He said, "He who has seen Me has seen the Father" (John 14:9). Jesus gave himself sacrificially for you, to restore your relationship with the Father and to live a life of friendship and partnership that accomplishes extraordinary things—beyond your natural abilities, talents, and resources. Learning how to receive God's love and tender embrace is a key to your success in life—along with learning to love yourself as God loves you.

In Matthew, we are exhorted to love God with all of our being, and secondly to love others as we love ourselves (Matt. 22:37-39). You cannot fully love others until you receive God's love for yourself—free of self-hate, shame, and regret. Learning to love yourself is a major step toward loving others and becoming a great person.

In the book of Jeremiah, God revealed to the young prophet, "Before I created you in the womb I knew you; before you were born I set you apart; I made you a prophet to the nations." (Jer. 1:5 CEB). God was showing Jeremiah his purpose and was empowering him to step into his moment and fulfill his calling. We also read of John the Baptist, called by God to preach before he was born (Luke 1), and of the Apostle Paul, who knew that God had a destiny for him before his birth, "... God had set me apart from birth and called me through his grace...that I might preach about him to the Gentiles..." (Gal. 1:15-16 CEB).

These men, and many others just like them, understood their calling and had a drive to fulfill that for which they were created. A timeless truth for each of us is revealed in these passages. Simply stated, we were created in God's image with destiny in mind. As you walk closely with God on your journey toward living a fulfilled and meaningfull life, you will discover the purpose for which you were created.

Sometimes, people realize their purpose early in life, as did Jeremiah and John the Baptist. For others, like Paul, the discovery may come later. Nothing is lost with God, and it is never too late for you to fulfill the destiny he has prepared for you. God, as the master potter, uses every success and every failure to mold and shape your character and move you into purpose. With God, your failures are doorways to future successes.

Your greatest joy will be in pursuing the very desires and dreams that have been inspired in your heart. God is not limited by your past or your present circumstances; your past is not a prophecy of your future. God promises to order your steps today, free from the hindrances of your past. As you come into alignment with God's purposes, your future begins to unfold daily. He wants to do a powerful work in your life as you embrace his revealed will. The plans that God has for you and what he wants to accomplish through you are perhaps even much larger than what you have envisioned or entirely embraced.

The Bible is full of examples of people who pursued their dreams, allowed God to work in their midst, and saw astounding things take place through their lives. Abraham had a promise that he would father a multitude. Moses dreamed of delivering God's people. Joshua aspired to inhabit the Promised Land. David envisaged a kingdom that represented an age yet to come. Zerubbabel imagined a re-built Temple, Nehemiah a re-built wall, and Paul dreamed of taking the gospel to the known world. None of these individuals were perfect, and some even veered outside of God's perfect will. Yet God did not give up on them, and they did not give up on God. Perhaps your last setback or failure is your opportunity for success.

DREAM BIG

How is Jesus leading you? What is your dream today? What makes you come alive? If money was not an issue, what would you pursue? Dream big, because you serve a God who loves to bless the imagination, creativity, and dreams of his people. To follow Jesus faithfully and fulfill your dreams, you must realize that opportunity and comfort are strangers to each other. Most people resist change. Most of us prefer comfort and security rather than risk. If your ambition or undertaking does not involve risky faith and adventure, it is most likely not the dream God has for you. The one who created the universe—who placed the stars in the sky and knows them all by name—likes big plans and big dreams. In some respects, God is like a coach who comes alongside you to build you up and encourage you to believe, sometimes quite literally, that the proverbial sky is the limit. Yet God is obviously much greater than a coach; he is the creator. The creator, as father and friend, delights in coming alongside us and encouraging us to become all we were destined to be.

Recently, I attended a conference in Dayton, Ohio and was reminded of the Wright brothers. It was just a brief time ago that Orville and Wilbur dreamed that the sky could be theirs and that man could fly. The rest is history: they turned their dream of flight into reality—from a bicycle shop in Dayton, Ohio to a flying machine on the beach of North Carolina—just a little over a hundred years ago. Today modern air travel is accessible across the globe, all because two men dared to pursue their dream.

As you follow Jesus, allow the Holy Spirit to breathe adventurous faith into your heart. God loves to bless your imagination and creativity. Daring to dream big dreams is an invitation to join the creator of the universe in his ongoing artistic expression of what we call life. For Christians, creativity, imagination, and courage to pursue the impossible should be the norm.

Walt Disney once said, "If you can dream it, you can do it. Always remember that this whole thing was started with a dream and a mouse." Over the years, I have enjoyed going to Disney World in Florida, both as a child and later as an adult with my family. It has been a place to relax and allow the cares of life to disappear. Disney's dream of creating a place for families to unwind and have fun together became a reality that has blessed millions across the generations. It began with a dream, a pencil, a pad of paper, and a mouse sketch! Indeed, if you can dream it, you can attain it.

Vision propels you forward into achieving your destiny. It empowers you to go beyond your present circumstances to realize the dreams and purposes of God in your life. When you involve yourself in something that is bigger than you are, you will also discover new aspects of God. He is often at the edge of the dream— at the edge of your imagination—bidding you to follow him across the expanse of creativity into the realization of your desire.

Keep in mind that every great success was, in the beginning, something that seemed impossible or daunting to the dreamer. Where would we be if the Wright Brothers did not dream of flight, Henry Ford the Model T, or Steve Jobs the iPhone, to name a few? What about the early apostles and disciples who desired to take the message of the saving grace of Christ to the known world? The list of dreamers who became history makers is extensive. Whether secular or religious, God is always inviting humanity to dream big with him.

DREAMS ARE POSSIBLE TO THOSE WHO BELIEVE

Jesus said, "If you can believe, *all* things are possible to him who believes" (Mark 9:23, emphasis added). Notice the *all* in *all*? Truly, *all* things are possible with God at the center. It seems with Jesus that impossibilities are the atmosphere for faith to thrive. Impossible situations did not intimidate Jesus, nor did he want his disciples to be so either; he wanted his followers to look at situations with God's perspective. Faith and expectation can change even the most daunting of circumstances.

It seems that Walt Disney had some idea of Jesus' perspective about seeing impossible situations change and dreams becoming a reality when he said, "All our dreams can come true—if we have the courage to pursue them." Courage is defined as "the ability to do something that you know is difficult or dangerous."[3] My perspective on the word courage is that it's a firm resolve to move forward to accomplish the goal or dream, despite circumstances being contrary. When you possess courage, you have the ability to face challenges and risks with a belief you can accomplish your task, goal, or dream.

Some people possess courage intrinsically; but courage is also an aspect of faith, which is a grace God imparts. It is a quality received from God, like wisdom. James tells us that if we lack wisdom, we are to ask God in faith for it and he will provide wisdom generously (Jam. 1:5-6). Just like we can ask God for more wisdom, asking for more faith and courage is a legitimate means of attaining it.

We see in scripture that courage and strength are qualities that God wants his people to possess as much as wisdom. This understanding was revealed to Joshua when the Lord told him to "be strong and of good courage" (Jos. 1:9). At times, what may appear as wisdom is actually fear, and it is contrary to God's faith-filled wisdom. The wisdom that comes from God is peaceable and gentle and it trusts God despite impossible situations. It is full of hope, not fear.

Fear can rob you of the courage needed to move in faith as God leads. Had Joshua yielded to worldly wisdom, rather than listening to God, he would never have led the children of Israel into their promised land. What about you today, do you have the courage to pursue your dreams, or is fear crippling you from trusting God and moving forward?

During an interview, Walt Disney said about Mickey Mouse, "He popped out of my mind onto a drawing pad twenty years ago on a train ride from Manhattan to Hollywood at a time when business fortunes of my brother Roy and myself were at lowest ebb and disaster seemed right around the corner." Right there is where most people stop—when they are at their lowest point, thinking that things are over—and they give up on pursuing the dreams God placed in their heart. Perhaps you have found yourself metaphorically in Egypt, like Joseph, wondering how you arrived there. You may question God, "What is going on in this situation?!" Or, in discouragement, ask, "What about the dream, what about the promises, God?"

It is one thing to ask God for wisdom during a storm; it is an entirely different matter to question God's integrity during a trial. Does Job sound familiar? If you are not careful, you can allow circumstances to derail you from pursuing the goal God has placed in your heart—or worse, you can become angry at others, at God, or even at yourself. Left unchecked, you may shut down entirely, and the dream will die.

I read an article a few years ago about new business failures. The data suggested that nearly 85% of all small businesses fail before they reach the five-year mark. Curiously, some experts noticed that many of those businesses closed just before becoming profitable. Success is often on the horizon of what appears like certain failure.

Here is something else worth noting: did you know that there is a temperature difference of only one degree between hot water and steam? I like a cup of hot tea in the afternoon. As the tea kettle reaches the transition temperature of 212 degrees Fahrenheit, the water boils and steam is released. At one moment, the water is just hot, but the next, it reaches the critical temperature and begins to boil. 211 degrees is not enough; it must be 212 degrees for water to boil. I wonder how many of our dreams are ready to boil—right on the verge of becoming a reality—when we remove the energy and heat, and the dream just stays hot, never boiling.

Do your dreams seem like a faded memory today? Perhaps there has been a setback in your life; some unexpected turn of events such as a job loss, an illness, the death of a loved one, a divorce, financial debt, or a bankruptcy. Maybe you have reached a place of discouragement and despair, and you feel tired, ready to give up. Perhaps you are wondering, "Where is God—is there any hope left of fulfilling my dream?" Hang in there; God will not fail you!

The enemy will try to convince you that God does not care, that there is no point in praying or continuing to work hard toward your dream. It can culminate in the ultimate lie: it is over, so just give up. To this, God speaks through Paul, "So let's not get tired of doing what is good. At just the right time we will reap a harvest of blessing if we don't give up" (Gal. 6:9 NLT). You see, it is a conditional promise—we harvest the fruit of hard work if we do not give up.

Honestly, like many others, I have been ready to quit on my dreams at various times in life. I have discovered, however, that by following Jesus what may seem like delays and setbacks are only opportunities for his grace to shine brighter in my current situation. Here is something else I have discovered as well: faith, courage, and persistence will keep you moving forward when everything else is against you.

STREAMS IN THE DESERT

We moved to Tucson in late spring of 2001. Coming from the east coast, it was a daunting yet exciting change for us. It was not an easy decision, as it involved faith, risk, and separation from family. After much prayer, Carolyn and I accepted the job offer in Tucson. The next day, God spoke something to my heart I will never forget, "Your family will flourish, you will excel in your job, and your ministry will prosper in Tucson—can I not make streams in the desert?"

God has delivered on his promise; we have witnessed his hand and favor over our lives, work, and ministry here during these past seventeen years. If that was not enough, we have also seen literal streams in the Arizonan desert. Every visit to Sabino Canyon displays the beauty of a desert stream meandering through the wilderness bringing life to plants, trees, and wildlife. God's promises, like a desert stream, bring life to the desires in your heart. Indeed, God can turn your parched dreams into living reality.

Within months of our arrival to Tucson, Carolyn and I sensed God wanted us to establish a new church here focused on God's presence, intimacy in worship, training for kingdom ministry, and a missional mindset to reach others with God's love and power. We began meeting in our living room, and soon afterward we rented a ballroom in a local hotel for church services. In early 2004, the Lord began prompting us to look for a piece of property to purchase.

Soon after receiving the impression to buy a property, God led us to an older Wesleyan church facility near the center of Tucson. The newly listed property was eighty thousand dollars below market price. Could this be God's will? Perhaps, but a couple of significant obstacles still needed to be overcome.

For starters, at God's leading, one year prior to this I had left the job that brought us to Arizona to pastor the church full-time. We were living by faith and drawing down our savings, as the church was not large enough to support a pastor's salary. Things were a little tight, to say the least. To give you an idea of how much we were trusting the Lord during that time: he would frequently send someone to our door with groceries.

Furthermore, we were only a two-year-old church with little financial history or money in the bank. I knew that unless some very large donations were received, it would be nearly impossible for us to obtain a bank mortgage for the property. At the time I was hoping for a "rich oil man" from Texas that would pay cash for the property, but God had other plans! By the way, never put your confidence in the arm of flesh—trust God instead.

Despite these potential obstacles, Carolyn and I went with a realtor to look at the church property for sale. After the walk through, my heart raced within me as the Lord spoke to my heart, "This is the building I have for your church. Do not look at the size of the sanctuary or the money in the bank. It is the building blocks, the stepping stones to the worship and revival center that I have spoken to you about." I felt the nudging of the Lord to write a letter of intent to purchase the property. Carolyn looked nervous as I said, "We need to make an offer on this property right away," as we stood outside of the sanctuary. The realtor just smiled.

Almost instantly, God gave me a gift of faith for the property, and soon after God gave faith to Carolyn as well. Carolyn tells the story that right after we saw the property, as she was washing dishes she asked God for faith to believe with me for the purchase of the building. She said that peace came over her, and suddenly she too had the sense that everything would be ok. We needed a gift of faith, as the property was for sale at nearly five hundred thousand dollars and we only had two thousand dollars in the church account! God reminded us, "Don't look at the money you have in the bank," so we moved forward in faith, trusting that God would handle the financial details. Sometimes all you have is a dream and a "mouse," but when God is in the details, the mouse might just be a miracle in disguise.

We applied for a loan at several banks, but none of them took us too seriously. Despite the fact that it looked as crazy as Noah's building of the ark, two local banks responded somewhat positively as we talked with them and applied for a loan. Yet soon after, they sent us very polite letters stating that we were denied. Bankers are great people, but they are justifiably cautious in lending money to people they do not know. Do the math: we were a two-year-old church of thirty people with two thousand dollars, wanting a loan for over five hundred thousand dollars— to a bank, the math just did not add up.

I was beginning to question God and started having some doubts about the plan. Human reasoning always questions risk inspired by God. Only with the eye of faith can one see the probable in the improbable.

I went back to God, the originator of this dream, and in prayer heard him say, "Fast and pray for three days and call those two banks again. Each of them will give you a loan, and you will be able to choose the loan that is best for you." The fasting and prayer was for us, not to twist God's arm into changing the situation. He wanted us to spend time in his presence, communing with him and meditating on his Word to build our faith for a miracle. So, we did as God directed, and for three days the church prayed and fasted, trusting God to handle the details.

After the three days, I called the banks back, and to my surprise (yes, a man of great faith) they were both open to taking a second look at our loan request. I was shocked. Not only were they open to the idea, but they were very agreeable about reworking a solution for us. Any trace of doubt was removed at that moment. I was now absolutely convinced, beyond my initial gift of faith, that this endeavor was God's doing and that he wanted us to have this building. We were simply walking with Jesus through the desert, waiting for him to provide the stream. He could have sent a wealthy person to pay for the property; instead, he decided that walking with him through the process would yield greater long-term benefits for us and our church family.

Within a month, the first bank gave us a loan offer with fair terms. We waited one more month to hear from the second bank. One morning, I was planning on spending the day praying and fasting for the funding. We were getting down to the wire for our funding to come together to buy the property. The Lord spoke to me that morning, "Today is not a day of fasting, but a day of feasting and celebration. For the bank will call you by noon approving the church for the loan." God then reminded me of Psalm 126, which would make a lot more sense to me a couple of hours later.

Five minutes before noon, the banker called to let me know that our loan was approved. The terms were better than what the first bank had offered, and—just as God had promised two months prior and again that morning—we now had loan offers from both banks and were able to choose the best one. I'll never forget that day—he specializes in the suddenlies!

Now that the first hurdle was overcome, we still needed to raise one hundred and fifty thousand dollars for the down payment. Almost overnight, God provided funds through donations and a couple of short-term loans. One of the loans came from Carolyn and me; at God's leading, we took a second mortgage on our home. You could say we were all-in and completely trusting God for success.

Within four months from the time we first saw it, our two-year-old church had all the funds needed to purchase this existing church property. By June of 2004, we closed on the property and moved our services from the hotel to our new church home in central Tucson. To say it was surreal is an understatement. Indeed, as is written in Psalm 126, we witnessed streams in the desert and laughter filled our mouths:

> [1] When the LORD brought back the captivity of Zion, we were like those who dream. [2] Then our mouth was filled with laughter, and our tongue with singing. Then they said among the nations, 'The LORD has done great things for them.' [3] The LORD has done great things for us, and we are glad. (Psalm 126:1-3)

In this Psalm, the writer describes the children of Israel returning to the promised land after years of captivity in Babylon. "We were like those who dream…" Like a dream, it seemed beyond the realm of possibility. When was their mouth filled with laugher? When the dream manifested.

We learned through this experience that it is easy to rejoice and celebrate once the miracle occurs, but it is an entirely different matter to walk in joyous faith before the promise manifests. This is where peace, joy, and abundant life reside—by trusting God through the process. Your ability to trust and partner with God through the unfolding of your dream is a key to living life as an extraordinary person and enjoying your journey.

FULFILLING YOUR DREAMS

We all have a primary purpose for which we were created. It is one thing to have a vision; it is an entirely different matter to move toward the fulfillment of your dreams. Here are a few practical action steps you can take on the road to seeing your desires become reality and becoming the extraordinary person God created you to be.

1. BIRTH YOUR DREAM

First, you must birth your dream. As is the case in any birthing process, it involves conception, gestation, and the actual birthing. The conception of your dreams and desires springs from your relationship with God. For many, this can take some time—perhaps even years—but do not give up. Continue to pursue God and seek an understanding of his will and vision for your life. After conception comes gestation, which is the renewing of your mind to think and see as God sees, and further develop your goals. Lastly, there is the final manifestation of your dreams.

Paul, in the book of Romans, shares the starting point for knowing God's will in your life: "Don't copy the behavior and customs of this world, but let God transform you into a new person by changing the way you think. Then you will learn to know God's will for you, which is good and pleasing and perfect" (Rom. 12:2 NLT). In Christ you are a new creation, with a new nature and new desire to live your life toward heaven, to live righteously, and to live in relationship with God.

In this and other passages, Paul indicates that you must allow your thinking to change from an earthly worldview to a God-centered worldview. When his Word and Spirit changes your thinking and perspective, you will then begin to understand his will and purpose for your life. A renewed perspective—for example, that all things are possible with God—is critical to seeing your dreams fulfilled. For some, this process happens quickly. It takes others a little bit longer to renew their mind, but transformation does not happen overnight for anyone; it is a process that unfolds with God over time. Enjoy the journey.

Psalm 37:4 says to "Delight yourself also in the LORD, and He shall give you the desires of your heart." Out of your relationship with God, a collaborative process is born. As you walk with him, your desires begin to align more and more with his desires. Because God has created you in his image and recreated you anew in Christ, you have the mind of Christ. If you are living in Jesus, you can rest in knowing that you are a participant of his divine nature and carry God's heart close to yours. God wants to bless your sanctified imagination and creativity and see your dreams come to pass. He loves your imagination and creativity; he is trying to help you unlock the fullness of your potential to bring his love and influence to many. I will cover the renewing of the mind in detail in the following chapter.

2. Does Your Dream Inspire You?

Secondly, does your dream inspire you? Do you come alive as you talk about it? Passion should be at the core of your goals, dreams and calling—passion will fuel your "dream engine." Often people choose careers based on the job market rather than what they think they will enjoy doing. Many find that they are unhappy or unfulfilled, which is why it is common for many people to change career fields two or three times in their lives.

For the Christian, your vocation—what you do to earn a living—may not necessarily be your calling in the body of Christ. Do not quit your job just yet but begin to focus on what makes you "come alive" in the kingdom of God. Eventually you may transition out of your job to something different; alternatively, you may continue in that career, but begin even now to focus on an area of ministry that you are passionate about.

Remember how Paul, who was an apostle and expanded God's kingdom to the Gentile world, also made tents to help fund his missionary endeavors. As Christians we are all called to be ministers of reconciliation and ambassadors for Christ (2 Cor. 5:18-20). However, this does not mean that every Christian is to earn their living by working for a ministry; this was never God's intent. We often have the greatest influence through living and working in the secular world, when we are in the world but not of it. Know this: your passion is quite often linked to the purpose for which you were created. You owe it to yourself to discover your calling, and then pour yourself into this endeavor.

3. DO YOU HAVE THE COURAGE TO PURSUE YOUR DREAM?
Thirdly, as I mentioned earlier, do you have the courage to pursue your dream? Walt Disney not only had to embrace the vision of Disney Land, but then have enough courage to pursue his dream despite the lack of finances and other obstacles that popped up along the way. Having a strong and courageous spirit is the hallmark of a history maker. Isaiah tells us that "Those who wait on the LORD shall renew *their* strength" (Isa. 40:31). If your courage and strength are ebbing, make it your aim to wait upon the Lord through worship, prayer, and meditation upon God's word. In this way, you build yourself up in the faith and courage needed to move toward achieving your dreams.

4. YOUR VISION MAY CHANGE
Next, understand your vision may change or evolve over time. Many people want what I call the "Golden Plan" before pursuing their dream: a set of plans from heaven revealing and outlining every detail on the road to destiny fulfilled. What I have discovered is that God does not send us a Golden Plan. Rather, he typically gives an impression or a faith-filled word of instruction that motivates us toward action as we follow Jesus. Often, that impression may not seem very "golden" as you wait on God. In fact, it may even look like fools' gold! Through an ongoing relationship with God, he reveals his plans to you incrementally as you walk with him.

God's plan usually looks something like this: "Abram...Get out of your country, from your family and from your father's house, to a land that I will show you" (Gen. 12:1). Abram, later called Abraham, obeyed God and as he set out with Sarah and their entourage across fifteen hundred miles of desert to the land of promise in Canaan. Guess what happened? Their dream evolved as they followed God into their calling. Eventually, through many interesting turns, God fulfilled the promises he made to Abraham and Sarah.

It says in Proverbs that "The king's heart *is* in the hand of the LORD, *like* the rivers of water; He turns it wherever He wishes" (Prov. 21:1). The road to fulfilling your dream is rarely linear; it is usually winding, bending, and much like a river with even some rocks in the middle. Know this: God holds the river of your life in his hand, and he knows every bend and every rock in your way.

Do you remember the story of Joseph and his dream in Genesis 37? Joseph's journey, much like Abraham and Sarah's, was full of turns and adjustments. He had no idea that God was honing and refining his character—reshaping the very dream God gave him. Your journey may take a circuitous path as well. God never gives you the whole plan because you probably would say "no" to his invitation. Faith loves the adventure with God. Embrace uncertainty and change.

Learn to value the mystery of the journey and be willing to allow for changes and flexibility in your dreams. I once heard the phrase, "Blessed are the flexible—they won't break!" That phrase is not in the Bible, but the implication is. Be willing to change, adapt, or even dream new dreams. Life is not linear. Life is filled with sudden twists and turns, even set-backs and failures. Keep in mind that the steps of a righteous person are ordered by the Lord.

5. NEVER GIVE UP ON YOUR DREAM

Lastly, never give up on your dream. Be willing to change, but never give up on the truth that God created you with a purpose in mind that only you can fulfill. Are you at a low point right now? Do your dreams seem like a faded memory? Perhaps you are tired and ready to give up. You may be wondering, "Where is God; is there any hope left in pursuing my dream?" I have prayed more than once, "God, I just need to know—am I in the pit, Potiphar's house or the prison? How far along in the process am I, God?!"

God is faithful even when we are faithless. On your worst day, always remember this: God's faithfulness sustains you, his love for you will never fail, and God will never give up on you. He has your future in mind and will work every situation along your journey for good in your life and to see your dream fulfilled. Simply stated, God will not quit on you, so do not quit on yourself.

Charles Spurgeon, a renowned nineteenth century pastor, once said, "By persistence, the snail made it to the ark!" Persistence will empower even the weakest of God's creation to fulfill their destinies. When we are weak, God is strong in us. Be persistent no matter what the circumstances look like, because God is for you.

Perhaps your dream from God isn't realized as you imagined. Never lose sight of the truth that God is always for you—no matter what happens. The writer of the book of Hebrews explains in chapter eleven that there are some who die in faith without seeing their promise come to pass. Ultimately, as a follower of Jesus, you are anchored in God's hope of the future resurrection and eternal life with him. Nothing, and no one, can separate you from the love of God that is in Christ Jesus (Rom. 8:35-39)!

Paul said this to the church at Philippi: "And I am certain that God, who began the good work within you, will continue his work until it is finally finished on the day when Christ Jesus returns" (Phil. 1:6 NLT). God loves to finish what he starts, so be persistent and keep at your dream, standing firmly in Christ regardless of whether it comes to pass. Jesus is enough—the fulfillment of goals and dreams are secondary to knowing Christ and being found in him!

CHAPTER 3

Restored to God's Original Intent

—⚬—

*"Therefore if any person is [ingrafted] in Christ (the
Messiah) he is a new creation (a new creature altogether);
the old [previous moral and spiritual condition] has
passed away. Behold, the fresh and new has come!"*

— 2 CORINTHIANS 5:17 AMPCE

*"By a Carpenter, mankind was made, and only
by that Carpenter can mankind be remade."*

— DESIDERIUS ERASMUS

MORE THAN A MAKEOVER

MY WIFE AND I ENJOY watching home improvement shows. One of
our favorites is *Fixer Upper* with Chip and Joanna Gaines from
Waco, Texas. Like many married couples, Chip and Joanna have
opposite gifting, but they make a fantastic home design and
refurbishment team. This show is especially gratifying for me
as I dislike remodeling, whether at home or the church. I am

thankful for others, like Chip and Joanna, who enjoy restoring properties.

What I do love about remodeling, however, is the finished product. I love watching, in hour-long segments, the transformation of houses that needed major renovations as they become stunning homes. If only we could have finished the last church remodel in an hour—sigh!

Whether it is an old house, an older church building, or your life, transformation does not occur overnight. Renovation is a process that unfolds over time. An old house is not a perfect analogy for the transformation of your life; you are *slightly* more complicated! You are not merely an "extreme makeover," but at the moment when you accepted Jesus' gift of grace, you became a new creation (2 Cor. 5:17; Gal. 6:15) which means you are spiritually a whole new person. You are daily maturing into a more glorious image of Jesus (Rom. 8:29) as you faithfully follow him, growing stronger and allowing the Holy Spirit to reshape your life.

From Death to Life

The Apostle Paul explained to the Ephesians and Colossians that they were once dead because of sin and have now been made alive through Christ (Eph. 2:1-3; Col. 2:13). Before Christ, you were dead; after receiving Christ, you are alive in him. Paul described this:

> [4-5] However, God is rich in mercy. He brought us to life with Christ while we were dead as a result of those things that we did wrong. He did this because of the great love that he has for us. You are saved by God's grace! [6] And God raised us up and seated us in the heavens with

Christ Jesus. ⁷ God did this to show future generations the greatness of his grace by the goodness that God has shown us in Christ Jesus. (Eph. 2:4-7 CEB)

To enter this new creation reality with Christ, you must begin by receiving God's gift of love and grace through Jesus. This gift is available to everyone who receives it and yields to his Spirit. Peter wrote that God is "…not wanting anyone to perish but all to change their hearts and lives" (2 Pet. 3:9 CEB). As you allow the Holy Spirit to guide you, you live from his righteousness, faith and love. Paul also wrote of God's saving grace:

> ⁸ For by grace you have been saved through faith, and that not of yourselves; *it is* the gift of God, ⁹ not of works, lest anyone should boast. ¹⁰ For we are His workmanship, created in Christ Jesus for good works, which God prepared beforehand that we should walk in them. (Eph. 2:8-10)

God's grace is not earned by your initiative or effort; you are responding to his invitation. Paul intentionally used the word *saved* here rather than the word *justified.* Justified speaks of being made right and put into God's family. The word *saved* has been translated from the Greek word *sōzō*, which means to rescue or save, to make well, heal, and to deliver.[1] Paul's use of *sōzō* implies that Jesus rescued us from certain destruction. Remember, before receiving Jesus you were dead in sin (Eph. 2:1-3). Now, made alive in Christ, you are God's workmanship, created anew in Jesus for good works (Eph. 2:10).

Workmanship in this passage comes from the Greek word *poiēma*, from which the English word "poem" is derived.[2] It is used only twice in all of Scripture: once in Eph. 2:10 and once in Rom. 1:20. In Romans, Paul argued that the qualities of God's creation testify to his reality, and leaves humankind without a claim of ignorance concerning God's existence. Now this creative dimension extends toward us so that he might create a unique poem through each believer. You are God's poem through Jesus—you read well. God did an artistic, creative work in you through Christ, like a musical piece or sculpture. His ongoing work in you through the Spirit—evidenced by godly character and operative spiritual gifts—are beautiful and testify of his greatness, wisdom, and glory (Eph. 3:10). His grace did it; you just said yes to God's gift and his power did the rest.

Grace is a gift which you cannot earn, but grace also empowers you to act. Dallas Willard, a twentieth-century Christian philosopher and author, stated, "Grace is not opposed to effort (action), but grace is opposed to earning (work)."[3] Because of grace, you are now able to take off your old nature and put on your new nature (Eph. 4:22-24; Col. 3:9-10). Your faith is demonstrated by your actions (Jam. 2:18), and your changed heart leads you to display your love for Christ and for others. Servanthood becomes normal.

God intends for Christians to walk in good works in two aspects. First, we display godly character through the indwelling nature of the Spirit of God. Secondly, in John 14:12 Jesus said that we, as believers, would do greater works than Jesus himself did. This means that we would do similar works of the same type as Jesus: healings, miracles, signs, and wonders (my books, *A Case for Healing Today* and *Receive Your Miracle Now* describe in detail the validity of the sign gifts, including healing and miracles). As you learn to rely on the power of the Holy Spirit who dwells within you through your union with Christ, both the fruit of the Spirit

(Gal. 5) and the gifts of the Spirit (1 Cor. 12; Rom. 12; Eph. 4:11) will be evidenced in your life.

TRUE FREEDOM FOUND IN CHRIST

I remember well the day when I first heard about Jesus. There was something in what Barbara said that was straightforward and inviting. "Bob, Jesus wants to have a relationship with you and help you become the person he created you to be." Then she just smiled and waited for me to respond. Barbara was the mother of my high school friend and an excellent cook, so I wanted to give her a polite response in order not to ruin my chances for free lunch! She was an amazing person in many ways, but in particular her faith and love for Jesus were genuine and persuasive; something I had never witnessed before. When Barbara shared her faith with me that day, it profoundly affected me.

Just before Barbara made this statement, I had been thinking to myself, "What's next? How do I move forward in life? How am I going to go to college now?" A few days before this conversation, my dad announced that he was divorcing my mom. I was sixteen. We were all in shock, especially my mom, who was now faced with raising five kids on her own. Barbara was someone for whom I had tremendous respect—she was always cheerful, positive, loving, and full of wisdom—so when she challenged me to consider faith in Christ that day, I listened carefully.

After thinking about her statement for a moment, I asked, "How do I have this relationship with Jesus and become the person he created me to be?" She then looked at me intently and said, "Bob, Jesus has known you before you were born and holds your future in his hands. He wants to free you from the pain of your past and he wants to show you how to live fulfilled today and realize your dreams tomorrow."

I continued to eat my lunch, pondering what she said as she cleaned the kitchen. She did not share anything else with me that day. At the time, I did not realize that this was probably the most important lunch meeting I would ever have in my life. God and Barbara planted a seed of faith in my heart that day and it quickly began to germinate.

Still, a couple of years passed before I accepted God's gift of new life through Jesus Christ, but from that day on my life was set on a collision course with the future. Soon after my lunch meeting with Barbara, I graduated high school and enlisted in the Navy. At Barbara's insistence, to which I am eternally grateful, she gave me a copy of *The Way* Bible translation and encouraged me to read the Gospel of John while in Navy boot camp. As I read John's gospel at night in my bunk, my heart filled with hope; I was beginning to understand that Jesus was the way, and the Father was the destination.

After boot camp, the Navy assigned me to an S3 Viking squadron in Jacksonville, FL. The squadron deployed onboard the aircraft carrier USS Independence. It was an older carrier, a "Forestall Class" of diesel burning carriers that were still in service after the Vietnam War. While at sea in the Caribbean, one night around midnight, I surrendered my life and heart to Jesus—I committed to follow him. I worked in an electronics repair shop and that night, when I was alone with God while test stations hummed in the background, I said yes to Christ and received God's mercy and grace. That night I experienced peace unlike I had ever known. Waves of his love and mercy flooded my heart. That evening on the USS Independence, I found true freedom when I met the Father's love through the grace that only Jesus gives.

The next morning, I was different, and I knew it. It was not until later that I would fully discover that I was a *new creation* in Christ, but the first noticeable change was the joy in my heart and the huge smile on my face. I felt different and my language changed. Others saw the difference too—both those who knew Christ and those who did not. It was not easy being a new Christian onboard a Navy aircraft carrier, but all the harassment was worth it. I knew the creator of the universe, the lover of my soul, and my life would never be the same.

In time, God began to renew my thinking as I read his Word and learned how to pray. All the changes God intended for my life did not happen overnight, but as I continued to allow God to transform me, my life significantly changed. There were setbacks along the way, when I returned to some old habits a few times during those early years with Jesus, but as I continued to follow Christ and allow God to renew and heal me, the old patterns were eventually removed. I learned how to live out of my new identity in Christ through the transformation of my mind. As my thinking changed, my behavior also changed.

That was thirty-eight years ago, and as Barbara predicted, God's grace brought healing and purpose to my life. I did not find religion. I met Jesus, the creator of the universe, who is the kindest, most loving person; who is intimate and real, a friend who remains closer than a brother.

Over the years God has brought many fulfilled dreams into my life, including marriage, children, career, ministry, and prosperity. Yet first I had to encounter the love of God and allow his grace to begin to change me—this was step one to fulfill the dreams in my life. It was not a one-time prayer or encounter with Jesus that transformed me; that was merely the beginning of a life-long journey with him. Transformation came through daily surrender to Christ and faithfully following him as a devoted disciple and learner.

Jesus is the "Key of David," the one who opens doors that no one can shut (Rev. 3:7-8; Isa. 22:22). He is the fullness of God in human body (Col. 2:9 NLT), the great I Am, the Prince of Peace and the Great Shepherd of our souls who walks with us daily, opening the path of life before us. He is the way and leads us to the Father heart of God. The desire of every person is to experience the love and acceptance of the Father. Your life, which will be filled with adventure and excellence, unfolds as you follow Jesus faithfully.

CLOTHED WITH THE NEW MAN

Paul wrote to the Ephesians, "...put off, concerning your former conduct, the old man ... put on the new man ..." (Eph. 4:22-24). Part of being restored to God's original intent for you is the clothing of your new person in Christ. Again, you are not an extreme makeover, but an entirely new being through Christ. It is an accomplished fact in Christ—you are a new creation and Paul is encouraging you as a follower of Jesus to "wear" this new identity. Paul says confidently to be clothed, or to wear this new garment. You have a responsibility to cooperate with the Spirit in this maturing process.

A paradoxical truth is that you are already sanctified and glorious through Christ in this present moment, yet you are becoming more radiant and glorious through the indwelling

Spirit. The body of Christ, his Church universal, is both glorious and is becoming glorious. This revelation to the follower of Jesus provides confidence to draw near to God unashamedly and have a relationship with him (John 15; Heb. 4:16). Remember, you are changing from glory to glory—not from being marred to having glory. As a believer, you are alive through Christ and partake of his divine nature and glory. You were a sinner saved by grace, but now in Christ you are a saint who is changing by his grace into increasing measures of his glory. You are righteous by his blood and presented faultless before God. That said, while your old nature has been rendered powerless in Christ, and you are growing in Christlikeness and his glory, you can still sin. God sees you as already glorious, yet you are in the process of transformation into his likeness and glory.

Ezekiel prophesied what God would do for those who allow Christ to transform them: "And I will give them one heart, and put a new spirit within them. And I will take the heart of stone out of their flesh and give them a heart of flesh" (Ezek. 11:19 NASB). Through the creative process of new birth, your heart becomes new. While you still have a carnal nature and therefore are subject to temptation, your old nature, with its propensity toward sin, loses its power (Rom. 6). Your new desire is to live from your union with God, led by the Spirit (Rom. 8:14).

Paul describes the increasing dynamic of God's glory upon our lives: "But we all, with unveiled face, beholding as in a mirror the glory of the Lord, are being transformed into the same image from glory to glory, just as by the Spirit of the Lord" (2 Cor. 3:18). The NLT translation of this verse reads, "...And the Lord—who is the Spirit—makes us more and more like him as we are changed into his glorious image."

A favorite passage of mine related to this subject is Psalm 45. The psalmist writes, "Listen, O daughter, consider and give ear: Forget your people and your father's house. The king is enthralled by your beauty; honor him, for he is your lord...He is enthralled by your beauty, you are glorious, gold is woven through your garments" (Psalm 45:10-11, 13). Jesus has made us glorious to the Father; the pure gold woven through our new garments is Jesus himself.

Do you have room for improvement in your walk with Christ? Probably; most of us do. However, you must remember the Father already sees you as lovely and accepted. You do not have to work to earn his acceptance or more of his glory. Learn to rest in the finished work of Christ and allow the Holy Spirit to change you into the likeness and image of Jesus. Learn to wear Christ and your new nature.

Do you have a favorite old coat you like to wear? If so, it is probably very comfortable and you are accustomed to how it fits. Perhaps it's a little worn and no longer in style. My youngest daughter gave me a stylish new coat for Christmas a couple of years ago, but at first, I preferred my old worn coat because I was used to it. It took a little while before I wanted to "put on" the new coat. Your old nature is powerless in Christ, but perhaps you still want to wear it, much like the old coat. You have a choice: wear the old or wear the new. For some believers, wearing the old nature seems natural, but this is deception. Learning how to abide in and remain in Christ is intentional on your part; that is Paul's point in both Ephesians 4 and Colossians 3.

As you read, meditate, and store God's word in your mind and heart, you begin to think and reason differently. This is what it means to wear your new nature. You begin to see from God's renewed perspective of life in this world. You start to think with new levels of faith, hope, and optimism. Your imagination and creativity begin to find new heights in God. Your renewed thinking creates confidence in God that is carefree and hopeful in whatever today may bring.

NEW CREATION REALITIES

God's original intent was that we, who are created in his nature, would walk in partnership with him. Humanity was separated from God at the fall of man (Gen. 3), yet before the foundations of the world were set in place, God made provision to restore his relationship with us through his son Jesus Christ (Eph. 1). God is not angry with you; nor is he looking to judge you or anyone else. Paul adds that God is not counting our sins against us (2 Cor. 5:19). Rather, he wants to restore his relationship with all of humanity (John 3:16-18) so that we can walk in his original intent. Jesus, who is the author and finisher of our faith (Heb. 12:2), expresses God's love, grace and mercy for humanity, and through him God is reconciling the world to himself whether they profess to be Christian or not. Grace does more than forgive you of sin. Grace empowers you to be a disciple, or apprentice, of Christ. Your new creation reality is expressed as you become a devoted disciple of Jesus willing to deny yourself and follow him daily (Mark 8:34-35).

The writer of Hebrews shares the completeness of Christ's grace toward us: "And I won't remember their sins and their lawless behavior anymore" (Heb. 10:17 CEB). Just a thought—if God is not keeping track of people's sins, perhaps we should not either. Mercy is superior to judgment.

Your new birth, which occurred when you put your faith in Jesus, began the process of the Holy Spirit's transformation and regeneration in your life. In Christ, you participate in the divine nature of God. Through his victory on the cross, your old nature—which was dominant before your conversion—is now rendered powerless and your new nature is preeminent. You are presently empowered by the Spirit to live in the newness of recreated life. Through an intimate relationship with him, we learn to rely on God to accomplish his eternal plan for the earth.

2 Corinthians 5:17 says that we are a new creation, and this could be Paul's most defining statement about what it means to be a Christian. Paul stresses that through Christ's death and resurrection, you have been united with him and elevated into his victory and ascension glory (Eph. 2:6). This new creation reality is an important concept to understand. You are united with Jesus in unseen heavenly realities, and you are enthroned with him in his victory and glory. You are now living as a new creation from heaven toward earth.

Translators have developed the English phrase "new creation" from two Greek words that Paul uses in 2 Corinthians 5:17 and in Galatians 6:15. The English word "new" is derived from the Greek word *kainós*, which means, "What is new and distinctive as compared with other things."[4] This newness is in regard to form or quality. The English word "creation" is derived from the Greek word *ktísis*, which means, "To make or create something which has not existed before; to create; creation (in the New Testament, used exclusively of God's activity in creation)."[5] *Ktísis* is the same word used in Colossians where Paul says of Jesus, "He is the image of the invisible God, the firstborn over all creation" (Col. 1:15). *Ktísis*, as used in the New Testament, involves God's creative activity. Thus, becoming a new creation conveys the idea that you are a new and distinct person through regeneration in Christ. Your present motivation is to live for God and walk with him in an intimate relationship.

UNITED WITH CHRIST

George Peck, the nineteenth-century author of *Throne Life*, superbly describes the believer's identification with Christ as three significant epochs: his death, resurrection, and ascension. He wrote, "...let us observe how surely our ability to apprehend the distinctive significance of our Lord's death, resurrection, and ascension—the three epochs which especially exhibit the completeness of His finished work—will determine the progress of our conscious spiritual experience."[6]

We have not only been made alive through Jesus and the indwelling of the Holy Spirit, but we have been raised up with Christ in heavenly realms: "For he raised us from the dead along with Christ and seated us with him in the heavenly realms because we are united with Christ Jesus" (Eph. 2:6 NLT). A better translation of "heavenly realms" is "unseen heavenly realities." Our union with Christ has ascended us with him into his heavenly throne room.

Your understanding of the finished work of Christ affects your spiritual growth. A person who knows they are united with Christ in his ascension lives differently than a follower of Christ who doesn't understand their position and authority in him. Those who know they are united with Christ in his ascension victory pray and live with confidence that God's power, through the indwelling of the Spirit, is active in them—right now, as a present spiritual reality—to affect change in their world. Operating in the grace and power of the Spirit is normal for believers who understand the completeness of their union with Christ and his finished work.

In Christ, our sinful natures have been crucified, including our previous passions and desires. We now desire to walk in the Spirit, following him daily and living from the revelation that we are enthroned with Christ. Our confidence is in Christ and in his power and dominion. As you recognize your identity and authority as a believer—that you are united together with Jesus in his ascension and victory—you will walk in the fullness of Christ, with the potential to influence your world significantly. Understanding your authority as a believer is essential to living an abundant life.

Consider the following words that Jesus spoke regarding prayer: "If you ask anything in my name I will do it" (John 14:13-14). Then in the next chapter, "Abide in me ... ask what you desire and it shall be done for you" (John 15:7), and, "Whatever you ask the Father in my name he may give you" (John 15:16). Finally, "Ask and you will receive, that your joy may be full" (John 16:24). Effective prayer begins with an understanding of our position in Christ and our authority through the finished work of Jesus.

My personal prayer life elevated to another level when I understood—not intellectually, but in my heart—that I am completely accepted and loved by my heavenly Father and that I am seated together with Christ in his victory. Christ took away my past, and it does not affect my current standing in God. I live now from my union with Christ and his identity, not my own. As Paul stated, "For in Him we live and move and have our being..." (Acts 17:28). God hears and answers my prayers based on my standing in Christ and my relationship with him as a loved son.

THE RENEWED MIND

As much as Paul and the other writers of the New Testament stress our union with Christ and the reality of being a new creation as a believer, they also teach the importance of maturing to become more like Christ. One central way God accomplishes this in your life is through the transformation of your thinking. As you allow your mind to be continually changed into the nature and image of God (Rom 12:2; 2 Cor. 3:18) you become more and more like Jesus, understanding God's will for your life with more clarity. This process of transformation through the renewing of your mind enables you to have God's perspective on life and empowers you to become the extraordinary person you were created to be.

Paul explains this process in Romans 12:2 (NLT): "Don't copy the behavior and customs of this world, but let God transform you into a new person by changing the way you think. Then you will learn to know God's will for you, which is good and pleasing and perfect." The English word "transform" in this passage, as well as in 2 Corinthians 3:18, comes from the Greek word *metamorphoō* which primarily means "to change the essential form or nature of something, or to become completely different."[7] In Christ, we have already become something new, of a different form or nature. Therefore, Paul exhorts the reader to allow the Spirit to change the essential nature of how we think as well; to realize this change, we must cooperate with the process.

I love watching butterflies. I tend to be linear in my thinking, so observing the beauty and random motion of butterflies is intriguing to me. During the fall season in Arizona, many butterflies—sometimes in large beautiful concentrations—are active and darting about looking for flowers or plants from which to drink nectar. When I see butterflies in flight, they remind me of the English word metamorphosis, which is derived from the Greek word *metamorphoō*. According to Merriam-Webster Dictionary, metamorphosis means "a major change in the appearance or character of someone or something. In biological terms, it means a major change in the form or structure of some animals or insects that happens as the animal or insect becomes an adult."

Biological examples of the process of metamorphosis include a maggot turning into a fly, a tadpole into a frog, and a caterpillar turning into a moth or beautiful butterfly. In this process, as the cold weather approaches, a caterpillar stops eating and seeks out a place to hang upside down and weave itself a cocoon. Within its protective casing, the caterpillar dramatically changes its body. It is literally digesting itself and recreating itself, and will later emerge as a moth or butterfly. It is an amazing transformation but notice that in order to become a butterfly the caterpillar has to cooperate with the process that God wove into its nature. It must stop eating, find a location to weave a cocoon, and then begin to eat itself into another form. Transformation and beauty are not always automatic.

Self-effort can bring some change to your thinking and behavior. However, ultimately, real change and regeneration are found through faith in Christ and the empowering of the Holy Spirit. Genuine Christianity, led by the Spirit, opens our minds to the potential of complete transformation. The goal God has for you is to think like heaven—to have a kingdom perspective in your worldview, to be conformed to the very image of Jesus. In the Gospels, we see the type of radical behavior Jesus requires—behavior that is impossible to live apart from a new heart and changed mind through the Spirit. Renewed behavior and thinking is a result of knowing the King.

While your new creation reality is a work of grace, the transformation of your thinking and the resultant changes in your behavior arise from your participation in the divine life with God. Simply stated, you are maturing in Christ through your lifetime, becoming more and more like him as you yield to the leading of the Spirit. When you live out of your new nature and identity in Christ, you begin to understand God's will and purpose for your life more clearly; your transformation enables you to see life from a different perspective, to live differently. You are being changed into an ever-increasing state of glory by gazing upon Jesus (Isa. 26:3; 2 Cor. 3:18) and as you reflect more of his nature, your behavior will follow your reflection. The Spirit is transforming you into the beautiful, extraordinary person God always intended you to be.

You begin to live life as you were created to be, free of fear and worry and full of peace, joy, faith, hope and love. You no longer live for selfish desires, but rather, you begin to live a life of purpose and service for others as God leads. Like a beautiful butterfly fluttering about on a sunny summer day, you start to fly, and even soar, moving with divine direction in God. Gratitude, thanksgiving, and giving of one's time, talent, and treasure becomes the norm for you as your life radiates the glory of Christ in ever-increasing realms of his grace (2 Cor. 3:18). The desire to reach humanity with the love and compassion of Jesus is a hallmark of a life devoted to Christ.

CHAPTER 4

Part of a Royal Family

—⁓—

"...you received a Spirit that shows you are adopted as his children.
With this Spirit, we cry, 'Abba, Father.'"

— ROMANS 8:15 CEB

"There is no friendship, no love, like
that of the parent for the child."

— HENRY WARD BEECHER

THIS IS MY FAMILY ...

A COUPLE OF YEARS AGO, the church secretary walked into my office unannounced with one of our single moms. The mom was overjoyed, emotional, and in tears. The secretary had just handed her a benevolence check to help with school supplies for her children and she wanted to thank me. A generous individual in the church had given a gift to help single moms before the start of the school year, and she was one of the recipients.

Single moms may have one of the toughest jobs in the world—the pressures of child rearing, earning a living, and providing a good home environment can be overwhelming. I remember what my mother went through after my dad left, and since then I have watched countless single mothers struggle in their journeys. Church, we cannot neglect their situation; they and their children need our help.

I assured her the gift was from the church and the generosity of others who made it possible. With teary eyes, she thanked me, and said, "This is my family now. I so love being here; this is my family." She left the church office rejoicing in God's goodness.

Family. The very word should evoke warm and positive feelings. Sadly, the reality is that for many of us it does not. Often, the thought of family generates shame and difficult memories. Many have come from broken homes and dysfunctional families, where there is pain and embarrassment over their upbringing and lineage. If you are one of the fortunate ones who had good parents and a healthy home and family life, I rejoice with you and encourage you never to take your natural family for granted—thank God for this gift in your life.

However, whether you have come from a good home with a rich family heritage or from a more challenging family history, I have great news for you: as a Christian, you are now part of God's family. God's family lineage begins with Jesus, in whom there is no sin, no imperfection, and who radiates the glory of God in faultlessness. The revelation of your adoption into God's royal family and kingdom is a vital step to becoming the person God ordained you to be.

AFFIRMED BY THE FATHER

In Matthew's gospel, we read that Jesus was affirmed and loved as a son by the Father: "And suddenly a voice *came* from heaven, saying, "This is My beloved Son, in whom I am well pleased'" (Matt. 3:17). Before Jesus performed a single miracle, God the

Father affirmed God the Son as a son. Jesus' identity is not in his performance; his identity is rooted in sonship with the Father, and as such he is a partaker of his Father's identity.

The Father has always wanted a family rather than subjects. Your identification with Christ as a follower affords you a place as a son or daughter in the Father's family. You are not working for his love and acceptance. No performance is necessary. Your new birth in Christ provides placement into the Father's house. Complete acceptance and adoption through grace is an unconditional gift. Good works will be the fruit of your walk with God—these things flow out of your confidence in God's love and acceptance—but they are not needed to qualify for your place.

Many today have never received the Father's affirmation. Experiencing God's love as his son or daughter is essential to breaking ungodly beliefs about yourself and dismantling "orphan thinking" in your life. It frees you from rejection and abandonment. Orphans tend to strive for acceptance, whereas sons and daughters in healthy families are secure.

How do we receive the Father's affirmation? I have discovered most Christians know this intellectually, but fewer experience the Father's embrace at a heart level. Love is expressed "heart to heart." The fullness of the Father's love toward you can only be learned as you spend time with God in his presence. As you allow the Holy Spirit to embrace and lead you, the love of God will fill your heart. You know you are child of God, not just as a revelation to your mind, but also as a revelation to your heart. Paul describes the depth of God's love for us and the completeness of our adoption into God's family in his letter to the Romans:

> [14]For all who are led by the Spirit of God are children of God. [15]So you have not received a spirit that makes you

fearful slaves. Instead, you received God's Spirit when he adopted you as his own children. Now we call him, 'Abba, Father.' [16]For his Spirit joins with our spirit to affirm that we are God's children. [17]And since we are his children, we are his heirs. In fact, together with Christ we are heirs of God's glory. (Rom. 8:14-17 NLT)

ADOPTED BY GOD

In Christ, you are no longer an orphan, a black sheep, or from a broken family lineage. Rather, you are loved, adopted, and an empowered child of God. Under Roman law, an adopted child received all legal rights to the father's property, even if he or she were formerly a slave. The adopted child was not second class; rather, they were equal to all other children in their father's family and had all the same rights and privileges. Furthermore, the Roman law specified that an adopted child could never be disowned or disinherited from the family. Oddly, in Roman society, a biological child could be removed from the household and inheritance, but not the adopted child. The adopted child was secure in their new family. Likewise, when we become a Christian, we gain all of the privileges of being a child in God's family.

Your adoption into God's family has given you the privilege to live as an heir of God, and as joint heir with Christ in the inheritance of the Father's house. Through your union with Jesus you can claim, with confidence, your inheritance as his child and the rights to God's promises and resources. God's love for you is complete; nothing will separate you from his love and you can find security in it. You do not have to strive to earn his love or acceptance. You need to love yourself as much as God loves you.

Paul explained to the Ephesians that we were chosen to be part of God's family: "⁴ Even before he made the world, God loved us and chose us in Christ to be holy and without fault in his eyes. ⁵ God decided in advance to adopt us into his own family by bringing us to himself through Jesus Christ. This is what he wanted to do, and it gave him great pleasure" (Eph. 1:4-5 NLT). It is a mysterious plan: before God created the world, we, who were in the heart and mind of God, were chosen to be part of God's family—like him, holy and without fault.

In Christ, you have a new identity and a new family heritage. Permitting the Holy Spirit to renew your mind to the truth of your acceptance into God's family and kingdom is essential in discovering your calling. When you agree with your new identity in Christ, you can begin to embrace the destiny God offers. Individual identity leads to changed behavior; changed behavior will lead you into a successful and victorious life.

Sonship Frees You from Fear

Your adoption liberates you from bondage to and fear of the law. Paul explains in Romans 8:15 that you do not need to be afraid of God as if he were a slave master. Placed in God's family, you have the full rights of his family, complete with his unconditional love. Paul also explained God's adoptive process to the Galatians:

> ⁴But when the right time came, God sent his Son, born of a woman, subject to the law. ⁵God sent him to buy freedom for us who were slaves to the law, so that he could adopt us as his very own children. ⁶And because we are his children, God has sent the Spirit of his Son into our

hearts, prompting us to call out, 'Abba, Father.' [7]Now you are no longer a slave but God's own child. And since you are his child, God has made you his heir. (Gal. 4:5-7 NLT)

One of the many benefits of your adoption by God is that you can be free from the fear of judgment. If you believe God is angry with you, you have not yet matured in your understanding of his love toward you or in your relationship with him. Nothing can separate you from his perfect love. John writes, "[17] This is how love has been perfected in us, so that we can have confidence on the Judgment Day, because we are exactly the same as God is in this world. [18] There is no fear in love, but perfect love drives out fear, because fear expects punishment. The person who is afraid has not been made perfect in love. [19] We love because God first loved us" (1 John 4:17-19 CEB).

God's complete acceptance provides confidence that in the presence of God you are free from the fear of judgment due to your past or present mistakes. As believers we are disciplined, but it is parental, fatherly discipline (Heb. 12:5-11). The shaping of your life by God, so that you mature as a son or daughter, shows you are genuinely born of God—he is your Father. God's grace is limitless, but the transformative nature of his grace spurns you to live a holy life.

This passage in John does not relate to a fear of judgment for sin; Christ removed the eternal consequences of sin. Nor is it about character development. It refers to your position as a child in God's kingdom. In the NKJV, the translation of verse 17 reads, "...as He is, so are we in this world." The Father completely loves and accepts Jesus—and so are you. In verse 18, the English word "fear" is translated from the Greek word *phóbos*, which denotes both the fear of terror and the reverential fear of God.[1] We are to reverentially fear and honor God, but not fear the terror of punishment, which was removed in Christ.

Let's for a moment consider the last words of Jesus on the cross. The psalmist wrote, "My God, My God, why have you forsaken Me?" (Psalm 22:1). Was Jesus forsaken by the Father on the cross? No, God the Father could not have abandoned God the Son, otherwise the eternal trinity would not be eternal! The indivisible essence of God cannot be separated. With that said, Jesus did carry our brokenness, rejection, sin, and disease upon himself on the cross, but in the presence of the Father.

When Jesus cried out, "My God, My God, why have You forsaken Me," he was in fact referring to the first line of Psalm 22:1. He used a *remez* to refer to the entirety of Psalm 22, as well as Psalm 23 and Psalm 24—the shepherd Psalms. What is a *remez*?

Have you ever heard part of a song and immediately completed or sang the remaining lyrics in your mind? Most of us have. Consider the patriotic song, *God Bless America*. If I began to write or sing the first few lyrics, such as "God bless America, land that I ..." most of us would continue, "love, stand beside her and guide her ..." etc. By just giving a few words of this well-known song, I have given a hint about the entire song and direction that I am going in communication.

This practice, not just related to songs, was common among early Hebrew students and scholars of the Old Testament. Before chapter and verses were used in the Bible, when a Rabbi would merely speak the first sentence of a psalm or key passage of scripture, people would know that he was now referring to the entire Psalm or passage. The Semitic term for this practice is *remez*.

Jesus was giving a "hint" on the cross to those who understood. He was implying, "look at Psalm 22, and the shepherd Psalms, I'm identifying with them!" Rather than sorrow, the ending of these

Psalms finish in hope and triumph. Remember, this is the only begotten Son of God, the beloved Son in whom the Father is well pleased. God did not reject or abandon the Son on the cross, and neither will the Father reject those who have received the grace of life through Jesus—we are united with him.

Rejection and abandonment are powerful emotions that cause deep pain in the human heart. If we measure an earthquake, the higher the number on the Richter Scale, the more severe the quake. If we had a similar scale to measure human pain and suffering, rejection and abandonment would be at the top of the scale. Rejection can occur through the relationships we have with parents, family, friends, associates, a spouse, or others. Commenting about the intense human need for love and acceptance, Mother Teresa said, "There is more hunger in the world for love and appreciation than for bread." Humanity avoids rejection and strives for acceptance.

Here is the good news: as a follower of Jesus, the Father can eternally accept you. You never have to experience the Father's rejection; rather, you experience the benefits of his adoption and the privilege of a relationship with the Creator. Through your relationship to Jesus, you will never be separated from God's love and presence—this truth must become foundational in your heart as you walk with Christ. Consider Paul's words to the Roman believers:

> [35] Can anything ever separate us from Christ's love? Does it mean he no longer loves us if we have trouble or calamity, or are persecuted, or hungry, or destitute, or in danger, or threatened with death? ... [37] No, despite all these things, overwhelming victory is ours through Christ, who loved us. [38] And I am convinced that nothing can ever separate

us from God's love. Neither death nor life, neither angels nor demons, neither our fears for today nor our worries about tomorrow—not even the powers of hell can separate us from God's love. [39] No power in the sky above or in the earth below—indeed, nothing in all creation will ever be able to separate us from the love of God that is revealed in Christ Jesus our Lord. (Rom. 8:35, 37-39 NLT)

If you live as a fearful slave, not knowing you are an adopted son or daughter, you will fear God whenever you do not measure up or perform well. Rather, you never need to fear judgment or rejection again, no matter the circumstances. Jesus Christ has eternally reconciled you to the Father. His unconditional love and acceptance is not based on what you have done or will do; rather, it is based on what Jesus did for you. Pursue holy living, but rest confidently in the finished work of Christ.

He took the initiative, broke down the wall that separated you from him, and loved you unconditionally. When you have completely received his love and walk in this truth, fear of rejection leaves. What a revelation this is; not from an intellectual understanding in your mind, but as a revelation to your heart and spirit. You love God because he first loved you. Your motivation to live for God flows from an understanding of his unconditional love.

Jesus is the way and the destination is the Father: "[6] Jesus said to him, 'I am the way, and the truth, and the life; no one comes to the Father but through Me'...[8] Philip said to Him, 'Lord, show us the Father, and it is *enough* for us'" (John 14:6,8 NASB). Jesus' ultimate mission is to bring you to the bosom of the Father—and it will be enough for you. The English word "enough" comes from the Greek word *arkeō* in John 14:8 and means "to be filled with unfailing strength."[2] *Arkéō* also implies warding off negative thoughts. The question many of us ponder about God is, "Does he love and accept me?" Yes, God loves and accepts you and it is enough when you learn as truth the totality of God's love and adoption into his family. When you learn to recognize the Father's embrace through your communion in the Spirit, his peace and strength will fill you.

FROM A DUMPSTER TO A PALACE

Lisa is a good example of living as a daughter of the King. Like all of us, she is not perfect, but she has learned to rely on God's grace to renew and empower her to be someone she was not a few years ago. Lisa, a wife and mother, experienced the devastation of divorce several years ago. Her divorce and bitter battle with her husband for their children left her depressed and without hope. Lisa and her husband together had built a successful contracting business with all the benefits that money could afford: a big house, vacation home, boat, and motorcycles.

Suddenly, the business went through an economic downturn. The pressure of the business and decrease in finances caused a rift between Lisa and her husband. He walked out on her for another woman, and though he eventually returned, the pain and mistrust were deep for Lisa and resulted in a broken marriage. The suffering for Lisa was excruciating, and she entered a deep depression. At this point in her spiritual journey, she was a nominal Christian without a firm confidence in God.

To break her depression, Lisa resorted to methamphetamines to help her cope with her pain and take care of her children. Pain seeks pleasure, and many who find themselves in addictions, as Lisa did, attempt to mask the pain. Her children, whom she loved deeply, discovered her drug addiction and begged her to stop. Her addiction led to tragic consequences for herself and her family.

Lisa began to "dumpster dive," as she calls it, to find things of value she and others could use. She told me, "One of the highlights of this terrible season of my life was finding Bibles in dumpsters. If I found a Bible, I always saw it as a 'sign' of hope, and I would never throw them away—I gave them to others who needed answers and hope."

Eventually, Lisa's drug addiction led to her arrest and incarceration for eighteen months. Just before going to jail, Lisa met Carolyn and me on a dirt lot close to our church, where we were feeding and ministering to the poor. We began to share the love of Christ with her in a non-judgmental way. In fact, Carolyn saw her heart for the poor and asked her, "Would you like to be involved and help us with serving the poor and needy?" Lisa wanted to, but she was unable to commit at this point in her life, as she was soon to go to jail for her drug-related offenses. However, a seed was planted within her. Before her incarceration, Lisa not only met us and began to receive love and hope for the future, but more importantly, she fell in love with Jesus.

Lisa went to jail with a new passion for God and allowed Christ to change her attitude and mindsets. In prison, her life gradually began to turn around. Her desire for drugs vanished, her depression left, and she now wanted to share her love for Jesus with other inmates. She became a model prisoner, in both attitude and action. Lisa went out of her way to serve the prison in whatever capacity was needed and became an example for others to follow. Correctional officers took notice, and God gave her favor in the jail.

God also began to work a miracle with Lisa's ex-husband, who began visiting her frequently in prison. After her time in jail, she reunited with her husband and family and became a member of our church. Her problems did not vanish overnight, but she began to live with purpose and hope for the future. She learned how to walk with God and trust him to restore what was taken from her.

Lisa eventually approached Carolyn and me about our church food pantry ministry for the needy of our city. At first, we had some reservations. We wondered, "Is she ready? Will she stick with it? Can she do the job of overseeing this ministry?" After praying and discussing it further, we decided to give her the opportunity. It turned out to be a very good ministry decision. Her love for God, people, and this ministry has impacted many. Over the years, Lisa and other volunteers have collected and distributed thousands of pounds of food—canned, boxed, bread, fresh fruits and vegetables—helping hundreds of families in our city.

Lisa is living in the realm of God's "palace." She lives with an awareness of her adoption by Jesus. Because of her renewed mind and heart, Lisa became the person God created her to be. She recently handed over the leadership of this ministry to someone else in our church, but her transformation and years of service has blessed many families. She saw the need, felt God's prompting to act, and she determined not to let any more time in life be wasted—she was going to "seize her day." Lisa's past did not define her future.

Proverbs states this truth: "For as he thinks in his heart, so is he" (Prov. 23:7). When you awaken to your new identity in Christ and recognize that you are indeed a completely new creation with a new identity, you begin to live differently. You have a new nature, a new disposition, and your inclination is now toward God. Your behavior will change as you allow your mind to be conformed to the character of God and his word. Lisa learned to live from her new identity in Christ; her thinking was transformed, her behavior changed, and then her life changed.

God does not want to merely change you; he wants to transform you. This transformative process began when you accepted Christ and his gift of grace by faith. The Holy Spirit dwelled in you and began the ongoing process of transforming your mind and heart. The transformation that God desires to bring in your life is far more than just changing your "bad behavior" into "good behavior." Sure, that is important to God and for you. However, God is after a total transformation of the way you think; that you develop a positive, overcoming mindset full of faith in God to do the impossible through your life. This can only happen when you die to self through the power of the cross of Christ and follow him faithfully.

You are part of God's royal family. You have a new identity and new family lineage. Your past is past. God's grace is a marvelous mystery; it transforms you into your original intent for God's glory and your fulfillment. Walk as a royal son and daughter, because you are one.

CHAPTER 5

Partnering with God

—∭—

*"...Abraham believed God, and God counted him as righteous
because of his faith.
He was even called the friend of God."*

— James 2:23 NLT

*"If you want to go fast, go alone. If you
want to go far, go together."*

— African Proverb

FRIEND OF GOD

THERE IS POWER IN PARTNERSHIP; strength in unity. When you partner effectively with God and others, you go farther than you ever
could on your own. God created you for relationship with him
and with others. Healthy partnerships bring strength, and it
begins with the Lord.

Abraham was known as a friend of God (Jam. 2:23) and this
is perhaps the highest honor anyone can receive. He was not
perfect in his walk with God, yet scripture records him not only

as God's friend, but his "friend forever" (2 Chr. 20:7). Abraham believed God's promises and walked with him faithfully, and this friendship created a divine partnership that greatly impacted our world. His life demonstrated that relationship with God transcends our failures. God chooses to use those he calls friends, despite their mistakes, to partner with him here on earth.

Like Abraham, God invites you to be his friend. Jesus said, "[14] You are my friends if you do what I command. [15] I no longer call you slaves, because a master does not confide in his slaves. Now you are my friends since I have told you everything the Father told me" (John 15:14-15 NLT). To be a friend of God is a privilege and honor, and it begins with faith in Jesus. Like Abraham, you are not perfect in your walk with God, but the cross of Christ accounts for your missteps. As you obey his commands and endeavor to stay close to him, your relationship will mature through encounter. As you grow in friendship with God, the evidence of your friendship will manifest. You will learn how to work with him in greater measures to impact your generation and the generations to come.

FAMILY FIRST

Having a family was in God's heart before he created the world. As Father, God foreordained that he would have sons and daughters (Eph. 1:4-5). It was for the purpose of relationship that God created humanity in his image. Learning to live as a son and daughter with God is our first priority as a Christian.

Intimate family relationship is God's desire for us, and through faith in Jesus and the indwelling of the Holy Spirit, close communion with God is possible. God's unconditional love toward humanity is the basis of our family relationship with him.

Partnership in doing God's work is important, but sonship and friendship are at the core of our relationship with him.

God loves you and is pleased with you just as you are. His grace empowers you to become more like him and to accomplish remarkable things in life; however, he is pleased with you whether you achieve "great" things for him or not. Your partnership with God stems from a loving relationship that is free from the need to perform. Remember, the Father was well pleased with Jesus simply because he was his son. While you should aim to live righteously and display excellence in all you do, you can also rest in his love, free from striving or the need to earn his acceptance. You do not partner with God to earn his love; rather, you serve God and others because you are secure in his unconditional love. Our fruitfulness, which brings the Father pleasure (John 15), is the result of our intimate union with him.

PARTNERSHIP NEEDED

God recognizes our need for partnership. Genesis records that after God created man, he stated, "It is not good that man should be alone..." (Gen. 2:18). God never intended for you to be separate from him or from other people. After humanity's fall in the garden, Adam and Eve "heard the sound of the Lord God walking in the garden in the cool of the day, and Adam and his wife hid themselves from the presence of the Lord God among the trees of the garden" (Gen. 3:8). Adam and Eve's sin caused them to fear God's presence and hide from the very one with which they were intended to partner. God, in his love, calls out to us just as he did to Adam, asking, "Where are you?" (Gen. 3:9).

Through faith in Jesus, you no longer have to fear the presence of God. Through Christ, you are restored to relationship with the Father. The original mandate given to Adam in the garden is restored to us in Christ: "Then God blessed them and said, 'Be fruitful and multiply. Fill the earth and govern it. Reign over the fish in the sea, the birds in the sky, and all the animals that scurry along the ground'" (Gen. 1:28 NLT).

After his resurrection, Jesus confirmed humanity's original mandate when he gave the Great Commission: "[18]I have been given all authority in heaven and on earth. [19]Therefore, go and make disciples of all the nations..." (Matt. 28:18-19 NLT). God has assigned his church to steward over the realm of earth—making disciples in every nation (Psalm 115:16). Our faithful partnership with God determines the level to which earth is influenced by God's kingdom.

No Longer Slaves

Here is the challenge for many Christians: Intellectually, most of us know that Jesus has freed us from our past and restored us to our original purpose. However, many believers have not learned how to walk in their new freedom. Some entered initial freedom with Christ only to discover later that they are still much like a slave in their thinking and actions. Those who are still slaves in their thinking, due to an un-renewed mind or unhealed heart, will operate accordingly as slaves rather than as beloved sons or daughters of the Father. Slaves are afraid to collaborate with God and others. Those who are free from a slave mentality walk confidently in partnership with God as his beloved children, influencing the world with his glory.

In Christ, you are no longer a slave or orphan, but a friend and child of God. You have been adopted into God's family, and your past is forgiven and forgotten (Heb. 8:12). Those who know they are adopted children of the King walk in friendship and divine purpose with him. If we are tied to our past mistakes, partnering with God and fulfilling the Great Commission will not be foremost in our thinking. This is not a condemnation, rather a dynamic invitation to be overcomers in Christ.

To fulfill your destiny, you must learn from your past failures and successes without being defined by them. Jesus defines your identity and success. You are living your life in both the present and future; your future is determined by your response to the present and your ability to release your past. Paul says to "forget those things that are behind and reach forward to those things which are ahead..." (Phil. 3:13). Your past is behind you, but your future is forward and full of promise as you walk in fellowship and partnership with God.

Do you recall the story of the Israelites in Numbers 13 and 14? This is an example of people who were blinded by their past, and therefore unable to see their future. God had already given them the Promised Land and instructed Moses to send in one leader from each of the twelve tribes to spy out the land before they occupied it (Num. 13:1-3). The twelve spies were sent into Canaan and discovered that the land was productive and had enormous potential, just as God had promised (Num. 13:25-33). Instead of filling their hearts with faith, however, ten of the spies were gripped with fear.

The ten spies responded to Moses by saying, "Who are we to do this?" The root of their unbelief was a slave mentality. Their reasoning: former slaves who live in tents do not win battles against giants who live in walled cities. The Israelites were free from the bondage of Pharaoh and Egypt, but they still saw themselves as former slaves and therefore concluded that failure was inevitable. In other words, their slave mentality caused the nation of Israel to believe they were unable to possess what God had promised. It was their false identity that empowered unbelief and allowed their fear to rule them. Unbelief and fear are debilitating.

Those who live from a slave mentality instead of a sense of sonship also see themselves as insignificant, unable to live courageously with God. The ten spies summarized their unbelief: "We were like grasshoppers in our own sight, and so we were in their sight" (Num. 13:33). Further, the Israelites assumed that the Canaanites also viewed them as insignificant. However, in the book of Joshua, we read that the Canaanites had just the opposite perspective: "We heard these things, our hearts melted; neither did there remain any more courage in anyone because of you..." (Jos. 2:9-11). In reality, the Canaanites were fearful of the Israelites, having heard about the power of God that was with them. Assumption apart from God's revelation leads to unbelief and fear. The Israelites' assumption clouded the truth. By the way, wrong assumptions act as termites for any relationship.

God invited the Israelites to partner with him to accomplish great exploits, but unbelief and fear robbed them of a great privilege. Except for Joshua and Caleb, the spies looked at how big the obstacles were instead of how big God is. They were no longer slaves in Egypt, but they were enslaved in their minds by unbelief and fear. It would be forty years before another generation of Israelites possessed the Promised Land. The unbelief of the ten spies distorted the truth and caused an entire generation to forfeit what God had freely given them.

Remember, in Christ, you are no longer a fearful slave, but an adopted child in God's family. Promised inheritance is for sons and daughters, not slaves. Getting free of a slave mentality is essential for you to move forward in life and appropriate your inheritance in God. Inheritance is forfeited through an unbelieving heart, but it is realized when God's truth transforms our heart and mind.

When God is left out of your reasoning, the obstacles will always seem greater than your abilities or available resources. When you look at the challenges—and opportunities—in front of you and say, "How can I possibly do that?" then failure is certain. What are you facing today that seems impossible? Which is bigger, your problems or God? Your resources and abilities alone will never move you into extraordinary living, but with God, all things are possible.

The writer of Hebrews states, "But without faith, it is impossible to please Him..." (Heb. 11:6). God specializes in overcoming the impossible situations you face—it just takes faith on your part to see the breakthrough. The Bible is full of examples of people, like you, who faced enemies, famines, and every type of trial imaginable, but overcame with God's help: "...for with God all things are possible" (Mark 10:27). Honor is reserved for those who trust God amid contrary circumstances to realize their dreams. How big is God in your thinking? Is God at the center of your faith equation?

ROOTS OF A SLAVE MENTALITY

The failure of the children of Israel to partner effectively with God and to possess the land of Canaan was due primarily to characteristics that formed a stronghold of unbelief and fear in their minds: negativity, false identity, fear of transition, and failure to recognize the will of God.

Negativity breeds skepticism about God's promises. The ten spies saw more reasons not to possess their inheritance than reasons to possess it (Num. 13:31). When people succumb to negative thinking, they will find excuses not to move forward instead of finding optimistic reasons why they can accomplish what is before them. Negative thinking distorts and hinders the faith-filled perspective that is required to receive the greater territory God is offering. The promises of God, whether in his written Word or spoken to you, are invitations to realize your future. Faith builds a foundation of hope that actualizes the promise; negativity erodes the foundation of promise.

The ten spies saw themselves like grasshoppers, and this false identity created unbelief about the truth of their potential in God. Distorted vision clouds God's solutions to problems. Facts are subject to change; faith does not ignore the facts but declares that, with God, all things are possible. A mind cluttered with distorted facts seldom sees clearly with the eye of faith, but the believer with a renewed identity and transformed mind sees the breakthrough spiritually before it occurs naturally.

Rather than embrace transition and venture into the new, the Israelites desired to return to the familiar (Num. 14:2-4). You will always long for the familiar if you doubt God's ability to bring you through the transition. Let us be honest, most of us do not like change, but change is inevitable to realize God-sized promises and dreams.

To navigate transitions courageously, adventurous trust in God is required. This courageous faith develops as you cultivate an intimate relationship with him. An unbelieving mind will always desire familiar patterns, "...the lust of the flesh, the lust of the eyes, and the pride of life" (1 John 2:16), over the walk of faith. However, the "just shall live by faith" (Rom. 1:17). Former lifestyles are appealing to those who still see themselves as slaves. New territory is for sons and daughters who walk with God faithfully.

After the Israelites had refused God's invitation to inherit the land, they acted according to their own will by attempting to conquer the land (Num. 14:44-45). They moved outside of the will of God and were defeated by their enemies. Jesus only did what he saw the Father do. You must live in a place of close relationship with the Father to know what his will is and avoid the pitfall of acting on your own plans. The good can be the enemy of the best. There are many good Christian activities you can put your hand to, but what is God asking you to do? Do not be distracted by the good; wait on God to reveal his best for you, and then move forward confidently.

GETTING RID OF THE SLAVE MENTALITY

Getting free of a slave mentality is a key to partnering with God and seeing his promises fulfilled in our lives. The slave mentality cultivates low self-esteem, fear, unbelief, and failure to trust God. It is the fruit of a mind that is unrenewed to our new identity. The slave mentality is anchored to our past and causes an inability to move forward in our destiny because of past experiences and present circumstances. It blinds us to the promises and power of God.

To overcome the slave mentality, first, see yourself in your new identity. How you see yourself matters—your future depends on your correct identity in Christ. The Bible is full of examples of those who missed their inheritance due to false identity, lack of faith, and underestimating the power of God. You are not a slave in new clothes; rather you are God's beloved child reigning with him presently. As I have written in the previous chapters, you are a new creation in Christ, adopted by the Father, an heir of God and a joint-heir with Christ. You are part of God's royal family and priesthood.

Second, live free in Christ. When legislation passed to emancipate slaves in the United States, they were still living in slaves' quarters. However, as soon as they heard the Emancipation Proclamation, everything changed. They were aware of their legal right to say, "I am free," and to act upon their newfound liberty. Believe in your proclamation of freedom. Paul stated, "So Christ has truly set us free. Now make sure that you stay free, and don't get tied up again in slavery to the law" (Gal. 5:1 NLT). You are free in Christ; live in your new identity and freedom.

Third, trust God to overcome the problems in your life. Jesus has defeated every enemy through his death and resurrection (Col. 2:15). You are united with Christ in his ascension and partake in his victory over every work of the enemy. The Father adopted you, and his love for you has no limits. As his child, he promises to care for you. You can trust God's miraculous power and rest in the finished work of Christ. If the children of Israel had believed God's word, they would have known the land of Canaan was already theirs (Num.13:2; Jos. 1:3). Learn to rely on what God has promised in his word.

Next, choose to live optimistically. Negativity will rob you of the faith and courage to appropriate God's promises and realize your dreams. Do not allow negative attitudes, words, or ungodly beliefs to lead you into pessimism. Proverbs states, "For as he thinks in his heart, so is he" (Prov. 23:7). Let the words of your mouth be life-giving; they have creative power, for the "power of death and life are in the tongue" (Prov. 18:27). Taking your mind off of negative thinking will disempower it. Live in your new identity and see yourself as an overcomer in Christ. It takes a mind fixed upon Christ to remain positive in challenging situations and release words of life that will shape your prophetic future.

Part of your positive confession is maintaining a heart of gratitude and thanking God daily for your blessings. As you choose to live in thanksgiving, your attitude will improve and be more optimistic. Paul says, "In everything give thanks, for this is God's will for you..." (1 Thess. 5:18). Gratitude creates an avenue for God's grace to sustain you in life's journey.

Lastly, expect God to enlarge your territory. God's kingdom is an expanding kingdom; growth is to be expected and God wants to enlarge your influence so that many others receive his love and power. While there are seasons of rest for us to enjoy, we also need to guard our hearts against complacency. We may become satisfied with a thirty-fold return, while the Father is trying to lead us into hundred-fold living. Do not be content with failure or in using only a fraction of your potential. Remember, God is the God of the second, third, and multiple chances. A casual observance of the Apostle Peter's life proves God specializes in second chances and enlarged spiritual territory—even for those who have failed.

Be Content, but Press into God for More

Failure is not God's plan for your life; neither is mediocre living. God has an extraordinary life designed for everyone. We are to be content in God (Phil. 4:11), but we are also to press toward the goal for the prize of the high calling of God in Jesus (Phil. 3:14). Paul told Archippus, "Take heed to the ministry which you have received in the Lord, that you may fulfill it" (Col. 4:17). You and I, just like Archippus, have a responsibility to fulfill the calling and ministry God has for us. It takes courageous faith, free of low self-esteem and poor self-image, to press toward our high calling in Christ.

Jabez knew that God had more influence and territory for him. He asked God to enlarge his border and to bless him, to be with him, and to keep him from causing pain (1 Chr. 4:10). Jabez wanted God's kingdom to expand, and God granted his petition because his motive was right. Jabez was not ashamed and did not feel guilty about asking God for more of his glory on the earth. God is longing to answer the prayer of those who have a loyal heart toward him (2 Chr. 16:9).

The Israelites were more content to wander in the wilderness than to trust God for the Promised Land. Caleb, however, was one of the two spies that lived from victory with God. At age eighty-five, he wanted the mountain God promised him and he conquered Hebron despite its giants and fortified walls (Jos. 14:12-14). Caleb was free from a slave mentality and trusted God for additional territory. Learn to trust God for things only he can do—that is faith. I heard once, "If your vision is within your reach, it is probably not God's vision." Do not be afraid to ask God for another mountain and more territory for his glory.

In John's gospel, Jesus' disciples also looked at their own ability rather than what God could do (John 6:5-10). A multitude of thousands were following Jesus, and he suggested to the disciples that they be fed. Philip calculated that even with half a year's salary it was not possible to feed such a large crowd. Human resources will not meet humanity's needs. However, a boy saw the same problem, but included Jesus in the faith equation. He gave Jesus what he had: his lunch, which consisted of five barley loaves and two fish. Jesus went beyond human resources and met the need with supernatural provision, feeding five thousand men that day, not counting women and children. Partnering with God involves risky faith—but when we bring him what we have and ask God to do the rest, miracles happen.

What is God asking you to do? Be obedient, no matter how bizarre it may seem, and trust that as he guides, he provides. His grace is sufficient in every situation.

THE GREAT RECESSION AND A NEW SANCTUARY

Do you remember the financial crash of 2008? It led to what economists have termed "The Great Recession," which was the largest economic downturn our generation has ever experienced. The housing bubble popped, unemployment soared, the stock market plummeted, and the banking industry was in turmoil. Many feared economic apocalypse. Amid this chaos, God impressed upon me and the leaders of our church to proceed with building a new church sanctuary. God's timing is not always our timing. Advancement and security can be opposites.

In early 2007, I began to work with an architect and officials from the city and county to move a street easement in the vacant lot so that we could proceed with building a new sanctuary. Everything was on track to complete the easement change by late summer 2008. During the same period, I had several conversations with the vice president of our bank about obtaining a construction loan for the new church sanctuary. Like the easement, the initial work toward that loan was going smoothly.

In early September 2008, the city, county, and church signed the paperwork to move the easement. The city and county officials joked with me, "We think this is a first for the city and county to work so efficiently together on a project like this!" We all had a good laugh, and I left the city planning building that morning thanking God for answered prayer and giving us favor with the government. Little did I know that the perfect financial storm was brewing in our nation.

The ink was barely dry on the easement papers when the crash hit. Like most Americans, I was in shock over the financial storm that blew in across our nation. In a moment, everything had changed for our nation, as well as for our new sanctuary project. I quickly discerned that the odds of getting our construction loan were now stacked against us. I called our banker and he politely said, "Bob, no one is lending money right now. We honestly have no idea when we are going to be able to lend funds for construction or mortgages. I'm truly sorry." We put the project on hold until after the holidays. During that time we continued to worship God, praying for his will to be known, and we enjoyed the Christmas season with our families.

In mid-January 2009, God said to me, "Bob, I want the new church sanctuary built." I did not hear an audible voice, but a firm impression by the Holy Spirit to my spirit as I walked and prayed around the church property. The impression to construct the new building was strong, yet my mind found several reasons why it was not a good idea to start a construction project. News headlines declared economic turmoil in the country. The stock market was still in a free-fall, with no bottom in view that January. In the natural, it did not make sense, but after more prayer, we determined that God was directing us to build this new sanctuary—despite the recession. God specializes in moving obstacles during the most challenging seasons.

Every lending institution I called for a construction loan said, "I'm sorry, we are not lending now." We kept praying and I kept calling. God wanted his building built. Finally, the Lord led me to a company in Michigan who was willing to fund our church construction project through the sale of bonds. The catch was that over a million dollars in bonds needed to sell to fund the project. We were optimistic and convinced the bonds would sell. They did, but not in our timing.

We started the construction project in late 2009, taking the step of faith and clearing vacant lots. By the spring of 2010, enough of the bonds sold to pour a concrete foundation for the new building. As bonds sold, construction continued. The walls of the new building were slowly emerging in the once vacant lot. The timing of the project was predicated on the completion of bond sales by the summer of 2010. Unfortunately, by that date only about seventy percent of the bonds had sold. The contractor could no longer build efficiently and within the budget without complete funding. The project came to a grinding halt in late 2010.

At that time, I went for a hike in the mountains near Tucson and asked God for wisdom and direction. The remainder of the bonds needed to be sold and additional funds raised in order to complete the project. A partially constructed building is not a completed sanctuary. To relieve stress, I was hiking quickly and crying out to God in prayer. I heard him say, "Bob, I want my building built." When the Spirit renewed this assignment to me, new faith rose within me for completing the construction. I kept hiking and praying—my faith was beginning to go to new heights.

I remembered the opposition Nehemiah faced with his building project—yet with God's help, Nehemiah and his team finished the wall around Jerusalem in remarkable time. You see, there never is a "right time" to undertake big projects for God, including church building projects. There is only God's timing and it requires a tenacious, persistent faith to press on despite the challenges.

We continued to pray and sell bonds, and we entered 2011 with hope to finish the project. Then, another storm hit. One afternoon, just when construction began to progress again, the contractor called and said, "Pastor Bob, I'm sorry, I need to quit the church sanctuary project. I'm going out of business." I was in shock and angered over the situation. The contractor had not been forthright about the project, but at the same time, the slow bond sales contributed to some of his problems. He, like many contractors during that time, ended up filing for bankruptcy. Our building was only about seventy percent complete and we had just lost our contractor. Once again, I was praying the "Oh God" prayer—a prayer of desperation without many words. Yet when we lose heart, God is still faithful.

The church board found another contractor. The new contractor quickly assessed the progress of the project and gave us a proposal to complete the building. The remaining bonds had to sell, and we needed another three hundred thousand dollars. That may not seem like a lot considering the scale of church building projects, but it was a large amount for our congregation in a city trying to recover from a deep recession. Somehow, God helped us to complete the project by selling the remaining bonds, raising donations, and borrowing short-term funds from private individuals. We worked with the new contractor in a timely fashion to finish the sanctuary by December. Our first service in the new building was Sunday, Christmas Day, 2011. Jesus had his building built! Within two years after the sanctuary was completed, we were able to refinance the church mortgage and repaid all remaining short-term loans. God's miracles never cease.

God specializes in doing the impossible. When he guides, he will certainly provide. He can take our weaknesses and setbacks and turn them into huge successes. In fact, our failures are God's stepping stones to success. "He raises the poor out of the dust, and lifts the needy out of the ash heap, that He may seat him with princes, with the princes of His people" (Psalm 113:7-8). You are significant. You are God's beloved child with purpose and destiny. Allow him to raise you out of your past failures and current limitations to do the impossible through his grace and power. He wants to work with you to accomplish the extraordinary in your life.

REMAIN IN HIM

Effective partnership with God begins with learning to abide in him. Learning how to remain in God's presence should be the primary quest for every follower of Christ. In John 15, Jesus uses the illustration of a vine and its branches to explain the need for us to remain in him: "I am the vine; you are the branches. If you remain in me and I in you, then you will produce much fruit. Without me, you can't do anything" (John 15:5 CEB).

Your born-again experience unites you with Jesus, but the value you place on your relationship with him determines how fruitful you will be. Friendship involves relationship—it is not automatic—and fruitfulness develops out of intimacy with the Lord. You can accomplish much in your own strength, but you will discover your greatest joy in your daily journey with Jesus. With God, your works will have a lasting impact and affect eternity.

Jesus said, "You didn't choose me, but I chose you and appointed you so that you could go and produce fruit and so that your fruit could last. As a result, whatever you ask the Father in my name, he will give you" (John 15:16 CEB). You should expect a productive life; he appointed you to this. Still, he primarily desires relationship with you. Love is the motivation and lasting works are the result of your intimacy with Jesus. Think about this: when your prayers align with his nature and will, you can confidently pray and expect answers.

This truth has empowered me and many others to accomplish the ministries and projects the Lord placed in our paths; the construction of the new sanctuary is fruit of this. As you cultivate deeper levels of intimacy with the Lord, greater understanding of his desires will illuminate you. You can then have confidence in asking God for the things needed to complete the task or ministry assigned to you. Assignments are opportunities for God to reveal his glory through you as you bear fruit and impact others.

ANOTHER HELPER

By experiencing grace in Jesus, we know the love of the Father (John 3:16) and our communion with God and others occurs through the Holy Spirit. Jesus is the one true vine, and there is no communion with the Holy Spirit apart from a life surrendered to him.

Jesus said the Father "will give you another helper...the Spirit of Truth...but you know Him, for He dwells with you and will be in you. I will not leave you orphans; I will come to you" (John 14:16-18). The word "another" in this passage is from the Greek word *állos*, which means: "one besides, another of the same kind."[1] At Pentecost, the Holy Spirit—who is another of the same kind or nature as Jesus—came to be with us and in us for our help and comfort. The Holy Spirit aids us just as Jesus would do if he was physically here with us. The word "helper" is from the Greek word *paráklētos*, which is a word derived from *para* "beside" and *kaleo* "to call;" hence, "called to one's side." The word signifies an intercessor, comforter, helper, advocate, and counselor who comes alongside another person. In nonbiblical literature, *paráklētos* had the meaning of "an attorney who appears in court on another's behalf."[2]

Sent by the Father and Son, the Holy Spirit, who is just like Jesus, comes alongside you to help you. The Spirit reveals the Father and the Son to you, leads you into truth, guides and directs you, gives you strength, and comforts you. The Holy Spirit wants to envelop you in his presence. Your Christian life is to be an ongoing experience in the life of the Holy Spirit; he cares for you and wants to be your best friend and partner. Daily communion with the Holy Spirit is foundational for a life of supernatural power and consistency; without it, it is impossible to attain the goal of a victorious Christian life.

Paul closes his second letter to the Corinthians with this benediction: "May the grace of the Lord Jesus Christ, the love of God, and the fellowship of the Holy Spirit be with you all" (2 Cor. 13:14 NLT). Paul uses the Greek word *koinōnía* to denote fellowship in this verse. *Koinōnía* is a word that describes a caring form of fellowship with God and with others.[3] Communion, partnership, and responsibility are other uses of the word.

In Acts 2:42, we read, "And they continued steadfastly in the apostles' doctrine and fellowship, in the breaking of bread, and in prayers." Here, *koinōnía* describes the family fellowship that is expressed through living in the church body. At the heart of your vertical relationship with God are horizontal friendships with others—the two are closely linked. The friendliness of the

Holy Spirit is warm and embracing, much like that of a close friend. God, through the Holy Spirit, wants to fellowship with you intimately like a family relationship.

Another use of *koinōnía* conveys the idea of partnership, and an example of this is in Luke 5:7. After Jesus supplied a miraculous catch of fish, Peter needed help bringing it all in and called to the other fishermen who were with him. Luke records, "So they signaled to their partners…" (Luke 5:7). The word translated as "partners" in this verse is a form of *koinōnía,* referring to the fishermen as business partners. The men Peter signaled to in the other boats were his business associates in his fishing enterprise. With this understanding in mind, 2 Corinthians 13:14 could carry this idea: "… and the partnership of the Holy Spirit be with you all."

Looking at the earthly life of Jesus, this understanding of *koinōnía* as partnership makes sense. In the Gospels we observe Jesus working hand in hand with the Holy Spirit and with the Father. He was conceived by the Holy Spirit, empowered by the Holy Spirit, and led by the Holy Spirit. Jesus healed the sick and cast out demons by the Holy Spirit. Jesus would not initiate anything by himself, indicating his total dependence on the Father and the Holy Spirit (John 5:30).

Another idea conveyed by the word *koinōnía* is the concept of taking responsibility for someone else. In Paul's letter to the Philippians he writes, "Nevertheless you have done well that you shared in my distress" (Phil. 4:14). The word "shared" is another form of the word *koinōnía* and carries the idea of taking responsibility. Paul was commending the Philippians for their generous gift for his ministry. The Philippians understood their responsibility to help Paul and took up an offering to support him in his ministry. This act also conveyed their love and care for him.

Therefore, 2 Corinthians 3:14 could alternatively read: "... and the responsibility of the Holy Spirit be with you all." The Holy Spirit wants to be your partner and assume responsibility for you. He is the one who comes alongside to help you, just as if Jesus were here physically to assist you. In fact, the entirety of God is expressed in the person of the Holy Spirit, who is with you and in you in order to assist you as you partner with him (John 14:16-18, 23).

If Jesus needed this ongoing partnership with the Holy Spirit so do we. The Holy Spirit wants to fellowship and partner with you—just like a close friend or close partner working in the same business endeavor. We are part of a family business called God's kingdom. As you learn to commune with him in deeper ways and allow him to take more responsibility for you, he will take a more active role in your life. That is what heavenly partnership looks like. The Holy Spirit is your source of strength, power, and wisdom—allow him to be your inner strength and helper and to aid you in the journey toward your calling.

CHAPTER 6

Forgiveness as a Lifestyle

*"But when you are praying, first forgive anyone
you are holding a grudge against, so that your
Father in heaven will forgive your sins, too."*

— *Mark 11:25 NLT*

*"Forgiveness does not change the past,
but it does enlarge the future."*

— *Paul Boose*

Forgiveness in Tragedy

On June 17, 2015, a senseless mass shooting occurred at the Emanuel African Methodist Episcopal Church in Charleston, South Carolina. During a prayer meeting, a young Caucasian man named Dylann Roof entered the church and took the lives of nine innocent African Americans, including the senior pastor, state Senator Clementa Pinckney. Police arrested Roof the following day in North Carolina and he later confessed to the murders, saying he had intended to start a race riot. The lone survivor explained how the prayer group had openly welcomed the young man into their prayer meeting that night. Genuine love has no limitations or prejudice.

It was another mass shooting. Our nation was shocked, confused, and angered. Yet during this tragedy, the victims' church and family members expressed forgiveness on a scale that few of us have known, or perhaps even thought possible. At Roof's arraignment, children who had lost their mother said to him, "You hurt me. You hurt a lot of people. But God forgives you; may God have mercy on your soul. I forgive you." Only a heart transformed by God's love could forgive like this—the depth of God's mercy and grace is beyond words.

The families of the victims in that Charleston church understood that forgiveness is foundational to the Christian faith. Amid suffering a horrific death on the cross, Jesus forgave those who crucified him, saying, "Father, forgive them, for they don't know what they are doing" (Luke 23:34 NLT). The religious leaders, crowds, and soldiers were ignorant, and it was from their ignorance that they killed Jesus. God demonstrates the depth of his love by forgiving us, and he expects us to do the same toward others. Had the Charleston families responded in hate, a race riot could have erupted. Instead, their sincere forgiveness in the midst of tragedy helped a shocked and grieving nation by demonstrating the depths of God's mercy. We have no room for hate or bitterness; we must live in forgiveness.

THE WAY OF FORGIVENESS

We hate injustice. Our human response to injustice is often a desire for vindication. We want the wrong to be corrected and the perpetrator punished. The reality is that in our world, unjust behavior surrounds us. Wrongs are often uncorrected and the guilty go unpunished. Even if justice prevails, many still carry unforgiveness toward those who caused the offense. Yet as those families in Charleston demonstrated, true love for others is expressed by extending forgiveness as a lifestyle. In fact, we are truly free when we choose to forgive. It is a choice, and the feelings will eventually follow. We should live and love through a filter of forgiveness.

The Apostle John describes love as the primary attribute of God's nature: "God is love ... he who loves abides in God's love" (1 John 4:8). Sincerely loving others and abiding in God's love hinges upon your ability to forgive those who have wronged you. We live in a fallen world. People do and will continue to hurt us; some intentionally, others unintentionally and often unknowingly. You will not be able to realize the fullness of your future while still harboring unforgiveness toward others. How you handle offenses is crucial not only to your life in God, but also to your personal wellness and health.

Jesus made a profound statement in Luke 17:1: "It is impossible that no offenses should come..." In this passage, Jesus is explaining that people will hurt and offend us in life, and our response is to forgive. The English word "offenses" is derived from the Greek word *skándalon*, which can mean a "stumbling block or a trap." *Skándalon* denotes the act of placing a trap in someone's way, much like the bait stick of an old-fashioned mousetrap.

In the New Testament, *skándalon* describes entrapment used by the enemy. In both the New and the Old Testaments, the real issue in *skándalon* is the way we relate to God. It is an obstacle to faith and hence a cause of falling and destruction.[1] Jesus was telling his followers in Luke 17:1 that obstacles to our faith and traps from the enemy will occur in this life. How? When people wrong you, the enemy will attempt to trap (*skándalon*) you through unforgiveness. When you hold onto offense and unforgiveness, you have taken the "bait" of his trap and you are caught. Harbored unforgiveness fosters bitterness and restricts God's grace in our life. The only way out of the enemy's trap and the bondage it places you in is to forgive the offender sincerely. Forgiveness is God's way of providing us freedom from the unjust events that happen in life.

In Matthew 18, Jesus told the parable of the unforgiving servant. Peter came to Jesus and asked, "[21] 'Lord, how often should I forgive someone who sins against me? Seven times?' [22] 'No, not seven times,' Jesus replied, 'but seventy times seven!'" (Matt. 18:21-22 NLT). Imagine Peter's surprise when Jesus told him that he must forgive someone 490 times! Theologians have commented on this number and suggest that Jesus may have been providing a positive counterpart to the boast of Lamech in Genesis 4:24, when he spoke of avenging himself seventy-sevenfold times.[2] Yet Jesus was primarily explaining to Peter, and to all of us, that we are to continue forgiving those who wrong us. Our human reasoning and desire for vindication does not limit God's mercy and grace.

However, extending forgiveness does not mean that we should not establish healthy boundaries or ignore the harm that others cause us. Abusive patterns must be stopped and care must be taken to prevent further harm, especially in cases of child, domestic, and sexual abuse. In the context of this passage, Jesus was speaking to the spiritual issue of unforgiveness—the bait of the enemy and the importance of forgiving others. Jesus continued the story:

> [23] Therefore, the kingdom of Heaven can be compared to a king who decided to bring his accounts up to date

with servants who had borrowed money from him. [24] In the process, one of his debtors was brought in who owed him millions of dollars. [25] He couldn't pay, so his master ordered that he be sold—along with his wife, his children, and everything he owned—to pay the debt.

[26] But the man fell down before his master and begged him, 'Please, be patient with me, and I will pay it all.' [27] Then his master was filled with pity for him, and he released him and forgave his debt.

[28] But when the man left the king, he went to a fellow servant who owed him a few thousand dollars. He grabbed him by the throat and demanded instant payment.

[29] His fellow servant fell down before him and begged for a little more time. 'Be patient with me, and I will pay it,' he pleaded. [30] But his creditor wouldn't wait. He had the man arrested and put in prison until the debt could be paid in full.

[31] When some of the other servants saw this, they were very upset. They went to the king and told him everything that had happened. [32] Then the king called in the man he had forgiven and said, 'You evil servant! I forgave you that tremendous debt because you pleaded with me. [33] Shouldn't you have mercy on your fellow servant, just as I had mercy on you?' [34] Then the angry king sent the man to prison to be tortured until he had paid his entire debt. [35] That's what my heavenly Father will do to you if

you refuse to forgive your brothers and sisters from your heart. (Matt. 18:23-35 NLT)

In our modern society, we do not sell people into slavery or place them in debtor prisons. However, in Jesus day, all who heard this parable understood the severity of its message. Jesus was using shock and awe to stress the importance of forgiveness. To owe a king millions of dollars, only for him to order that everything you own be sold and you and your family be placed into slavery to pay for the debt, would have gripped the reader with fear. The debt was so large that it would have taken this man thousands of years to repay. There was simply no way to work it off in his lifetime; it was a life sentence of torment with no hope of getting out of prison.

The man pleaded with the king for mercy, even stating that he would repay the debt, which would have been impossible. The king had compassion on him and forgave his unpayable debt. Once again, the reader in Jesus' day would have known how astounding this act of compassion and mercy was. Sadly, the man did not extend the same mercy to his fellow servant, who owed him just a few months of wages. He grabbed the other servant by the throat and threatened him with debtor prison. The servant begged for mercy, but the man threw him into prison until he could repay what he owed.

When other servants informed the king of this injustice and the man forgiven of the tremendous debt stood before the angry king to explain his actions, the king reminded him of the compassion he had showed him. He explained to the man that he should have extended the same mercy he had received to his fellow servant, forgiving him of his debt. Consequently, the king sent the man to prison to be tortured until he could repay the debt. In other words, Jesus summarized the gravity of this story by stating that our heavenly Father will allow each of us to be tormented if we do not sincerely forgive others. Forgiveness is not optional with God—it is foundational to our relationship with him and with each other.

Sir, Your Van was Stolen

In the mid-90's, Carolyn and I led a mission trip to Guatemala with a group of youth from our church in Daytona, Florida. We helped build a school, ministered in church services and served the village children. In many respects, it was a fruitful and fulfilling ministry trip. We arrived home on a Saturday night at midnight, excited to share in our home church the next morning about what God had done on the trip. As we arrived home from the airport and pulled into the driveway with our rental car, I noticed that our family minivan was gone. I asked Carolyn, "Did you let someone from the church borrow our van while we were gone?" She quickly responded, "No, I didn't." We sat there confused for a minute—then an anxious thought flashed through my mind, "Our van has been stolen!"

We quickly unloaded the car and got everything inside. I called the police department only to be placed on hold for what seemed like an eternity. Finally, at about 12:45AM a police representative let me know both the good and bad news. "Mr. Sawvelle, your van was stolen a few days ago. That is the bad news. The good news is that your van was recovered by our department and is being held in the Daytona Police impound yard. You can pick up your van on Monday. Oh, and you will need your driver's license and a money order or cashier's check for $175 to have the van released. I also need to let you know that the van was severly damaged during the theft." I was shocked, frustrated, and angry.

I was so angry over what had happened that I could hardly sleep. A few hours later when the alarm went off to get ready for church, I was despondent and full of worry over the van. I lost my joy and peace and let the problem become bigger than God. Carolyn tried to help my mood and put everything in perspective, but all I could focus on was the injustice of the situation.

We arrived at the church and the senior pastor joyfully greeted us. He was excited to hear about our mission trip and the stories I would share with the congregation. Instead of joining in his excitement, I began my bitter diatribe about the van. Rather than remaining positive and focusing on the fact that the van was recovered, I was angered and worried about the damage that had been done to it. He quickly discerned that I was in no frame of mind to share with the congregation that morning. I had allowed the situation to rob me of the opportunity to share with our church family about the success of the mission trip. I was miserable during the church service and the rest of that Sunday. I was only thinking about Monday morning and getting the van back.

On Monday morning, I called the police department once more before going to the impound lot. The detective assigned to the case informed me that there was nothing he could do about the impound fee. He then proceeded to tell me the man who stole the van was in jail but would soon be released—even though he had prior offenses—because the van was parked when they had found him. Had they caught him driving it, he would have been charged with grand theft auto—a felony—but because the vehicle was not moving, they could not charge him with a crime.

Frustrated and angry at the injustice, I went to the bank and got a money order for the $175. It was a significant amount of money for us at that time. I paid the fee at the impound lot, signed the paperwork, and proceeded to the back of the lot to pick up the van. As I walked toward the van, my heart sank; the driver side window was shattered. As I looked inside, I saw a burned dashboard and damaged steering column. Garbage and clothes were strewn throughout the van, and it smelled terrible. Upon closer inspection, I realized some of the clothes still had tags on them and I concluded they were stolen goods. Sarcastically, I said to myself, "Just great."

I started the van and began my trip across town to the Dodge dealer for the repairs. I left the impound lot infuriated and wanted the man who caused all of this to rot in jail. I wanted justice—I had moved from grace to the law. I pulled up to a stop light, and while waiting for the light to change, I noticed an ashtray filled with ashes on the floor, along with something else: a crack pipe with crack cocaine still in it! I could not believe it. Visions flashed across my mind of the police pulling me over and arresting me in my own vehicle for someone else's drugs and crimes! My anger went to new heights; I was a volcano ready to erupt.

A few minutes later, while I was still fuming over the situation, something remarkable occurred—God gave me his thoughts for the man and the situation. Honestly, at that moment I was not praying. I was thinking about how I could get justice. However, God interrupted my thoughts and said to me, "Bob, I care very much for this man who stole your van, just like I care for you and forgive you of your wrongs. He is troubled and confused. Would you forgive him and would you pray for him to open his heart to me?"

My heart instantly changed. I said, "Yes Lord, I forgive him. Forgive me for having unforgiveness toward him and wanting vindication. Please forgive him and surround him with your presence so that he could say yes to you." When this happened, my emotions immediately went from hateful anger to love and compassion for the man—I saw him in my mind's eye, miserable and confused in the jail cell. Whether literally or metaphorically, many are imprisoned due to poor choices and need God's grace and our forgiveness to help set them free.

I kept praying for him while I drove to the repair shop, and soon I was back to worshipping and praising God. The tormenting thoughts were gone, and peace began to return. My thoughts were on the Lord, his grace and his goodness, and no longer on vindication. By the time I arrived at the car dealer, my heart was filled with God's presence and joy. The attendant checking in my van for the repairs must have thought I was a little strange as I brought in the vehicle with a huge smile on my face! A couple of days later, I picked up our restored van. It looked brand new— what seemed hopeless was now radiant.

I never met the man who stole our van. The detective called me a few weeks later to inform me that he had been released from jail. Over the next few months, whenever he came to mind, I continued to pray for him. Perhaps I will meet him one day on the other side of eternity. God is just, but God is first merciful and compassionate. Mercy triumphs over judgment. We all need God's grace, for without it we all deserve an eternal prison.

ASPECTS OF FORGIVENESS

Through Jesus Christ, God's love, grace, and mercy were extended to humanity. By placing our faith in him we can receive God's gift of grace and forgiveness for our sin—a debt that we could never repay. Paul tells us that our complete salvation (forgiveness, healing, and deliverance) is found through God's grace and our faith, not in exerting religious effort to satisfy the debt of sin (Eph. 2:8-9). Like the king in the parable of the unforgiving servant, God has extended mercy to us, not giving us what we deserve, but rather grace that has reconciled us to himself. It is this grace that is recreating us into the image and nature of Christ.

The word "grace" comes from the Greek *cháris* meaning benefit, favor, or gift.[3] Grace is getting something we *do not* deserve, while mercy is *not* getting what we *do* deserve. Grace is also, however, a divine empowerment. It is both an invitation by God to walk in love and forgiveness for others—even when they do not deserve it or have not asked for it—as well as the empowerment to do so and to overcome our human nature, which wants justice and vindication.

Many wrongly believe that forgiving others of the wrongs they have committed will excuse them of their mistakes. Their logic goes something like this: "Well if I forgive them it's like letting them go free, unpunished—so I can never forgive them." It can be difficult for them to forgive because of the pain and hurt they still carry, and it feels like it is their right to hold onto the offense. In this case they wrongly believe that by not forgiving and holding a grudge toward those who hurt them, they are punishing or executing vengeance on the offender. Their subconscious goal is to receive justice. Yet most of the time the perpetrator is not even aware of the bitterness directed toward them.

As Jesus explained in Matthew 18, what happens with this type of behavior is that the person holding onto unforgiveness actually imprisons himself or herself into bitterness, rather than hurting the one who offended them. Bitterness can even lead to serious physical ailments. The truth is that your choice to forgive releases you—the one who has been wronged—from the prison of unforgiveness. Time is not a healer; it merely masks the pain that many carry deep in their hearts. Healing begins with forgiving those who have hurt you.

Each person is accountable for their wrongs and actions, and judgement belongs to God, not with you. God is merciful and compassionate, forgiving everyone who asks of him, and our role is to share that which we have received. Forgiving others restores you to a right relationship with the Father and the river of his grace.

Some, however, also mistakenly believe that if they forgive someone, that means they must restore relationship with the person. Jesus said we must forgive and we are to endeavor to live at peace with others (Eph. 4:3), but this does not mean that all relationships can or will be restored. For example, you may need to forgive someone who passed away or someone who has been incarcerated for a criminal offense. If a family member or friend molested your children, healthy boundaries need to be reestablished for the safety of your children or others involved. Another example could be that of a business associate who lied about business affairs or fraudulently wronged you. All of these people need to be forgiven, but reestablishing relationship, or the level of relationship that existed before the wrong occurred, may not be possible or healthy in some cases. In other words, forgiveness is mandatory, but the restoration of relationship is conditional.

Initially, you may not feel like forgiving someone who has hurt and wronged you, but you must do so. Forgiveness is a choice, not a feeling—your feelings will eventually follow your choice. As you choose to forgive others, God will empower you to release them from the harm they caused you. His grace will begin to heal the hurt in your heart toward those who have wronged you. Mercy and grace are core attributes of our loving Father; learning to live a life of forgiveness empowers us to live in his compassion and grace.

ARTHRITIS AND FORGIVENESS

While praying for the sick after a service, a woman approached me asking for prayer due to severe arthritis in her hands. She was a middle-aged woman who looked to be in good health—except for her clenched, pain-filled hands. I asked her how long she had the pain and clenching of her hands, and she told me it had been about five years. I then asked her if anything significant happened five years prior when these symptoms began. Her facial countenance changed as she explained how her husband left her for another woman, and how her pain began soon after. I asked her if she had forgiven her ex-husband and the other woman, and she said, "No, I haven't, and I don't think I will ever be able to forgive them."

I then shared with her the necessity of forgiveness. By forgiving her husband and this other woman, it did not excuse them of the wrong, but it would release her from the torment of unforgiveness. I also explained to her that forgiveness was a choice, an act of obedience to God's directive, and that by letting them go God would begin to heal the hurt in her heart.

She agreed and allowed me to lead her in a prayer of forgiveness for them. As she prayed with me, tears began to flow from her eyes. I then prayed for her hands to be healed of the clenching and for the pain to go. Less than a minute later, she could freely move her hands—there was no more clenching, and all the pain was gone. Jesus healed her hands, but first he began to heal her heart of the pain caused by her former husband and the other woman. Her healing began when she chose to forgive. Forgiveness is a choice, not a feeling.

According to Dr. Loring T. Swaim, author of *Arthritis, Medicine, and Spiritual Laws*, a major cause of arthritis is unresolved negative emotions and anger.[4] Proverbs also describes the effect of anger and negative emotions: "A peaceful mind gives life to the body, but jealousy rots the bones" (Prov. 14:30 CEB). Anger, bitterness, and unresolved negative emotions can lead to detrimental health issues—not the least of which is arthritis. Most people involved with healing ministry are aware of this reality.

I remember watching many years ago a teaching about forgiveness and bitterness by Derek Prince, a respected Bible teacher from the twentieth century. Prince believed and taught that nearly all arthritis and joint pain was a result of someone's lack of forgiveness toward others. Unresolved unforgiveness becomes bitterness and can cause severe arthritic or other conditions. After leading people through prayers of forgiveness, he would commonly say a corporate prayer for all in attendance for the healing of arthritis, with remarkable success in his ministry.

FORGIVENESS AND JUDGMENTS

Forgiveness is like a coin. It has two sides with different engravings, but they are both part of the same coin. On one side is forgiveness, and on the other side is judgment. When talking to individuals about forgiveness, I frequently discern that they have not fully forgiven others who have wronged them. When I ask them, "Have you completely forgiven the other person?" they might say, "Oh yes, I forgave them already." Yet when I follow with another question— "Did you break your agreement with any judgments you have toward them?"—the response varies. Often they will say something like, "No, I haven't. I'm not sure what that means."

Passing judgment on someone is like making a predetermination about who that person is, including their character or the motives behind their actions, prior to knowing the actual details or facts. In Matthew 7:1-2, Jesus stated, "[1] Don't judge, so that you won't be judged. [2] You'll receive the same judgment you give. Whatever you deal out will be dealt out to you" (CEB). The danger for you is this: you can say you forgave someone, but if you are judging the person based on their actions, you risk being judged, or having judgment dealt back to you, by the same standard. For example, if I judge my dad as being a poor father because of a certain behavior, I run the risk of reaping (or having dealt back to me) that same behavior in my life.

No parent is perfect. The behaviors of both good and bad parents can cause hurts and judgments in the hearts of their children. In order to walk in complete freedom and victory you must forgive and break judgments toward anyone who has hurt you, and this includes your parents. Judgments against your parents may sound like this, "Well if my dad were a good father, he wouldn't have left us." Alternatively, "If my mom were a good mother, she would not have yelled at me all the time." These are just two examples among many. It is possible to forgive your parent(s) for their actions, but still judge them as not being a good parent because of their poor parenting skills or bad choices they made in life. The result is that you have not truly forgiven them, and you are now likely to reap the same type of behavior patterns as your parent(s). This principle applies to anyone who has wronged you.

When you do not measure others by the same standard of mercy that you desire for yourself, you empower the enemy to torment you and to reap the same type of behavior with which you are judging the other person. You are operating in the law, or legalism, and not in grace. Grace is superior to the law.

Jesus not only forgave those who were crucifying him, but he released them of judgments: "Father, forgive them; for they do not know what they are doing" (Luke 23:34). He knew that their ignorance and fallen nature were factors in their behavior, and that unseen spiritual forces were at work. All of us make poor decisions at times, including those who are closest to us. We often judge the behavior of others without understanding the factors behind their incorrect behavior.

Jesus said, "Whenever you stand praying, forgive, if you have anything against anyone; so that your Father in heaven may also forgive you your trespasses" (Mark 11:25-26). Your prayers will be more effective when you pray with a heart of forgiveness toward others. As you forgive them, you abide in the overflow of God's marvelous grace and forgiveness. Your wellness and destiny depend on your ability to forgive others unconditionally.

DEAF MUTE HEALED AFTER FORGIVING MOTHER

One of the most dramatic cases of unforgiveness and judgments I have observed occurred on a ministry trip to Brazil several years ago when I prayed for a young woman who was struggling to forgive her parent. She was eighteen years old and was born deaf and mute. Her doctor brought her to one of our meetings and asked me to pray that she would be healed of her deaf and mute condition. She knew the young lady and her family intimately for many years. I and another member on our ministry team began to pray with this young lady and her doctor for her healing. We prayed for several minutes with no indication of change.

I asked the doctor about the girl's father and whether he was in her life, etc. The doctor explained that soon after she was born, her father left as he could not deal with the condition of his daughter. The young woman's mother raised her by herself. We then asked the young lady if she had any unforgiveness toward her father for leaving. To my surprise, she communicated through sign language via the doctor that she held no ill feelings toward her father.

The doctor then told me to ask how she felt about her mother. As the doctor communicated to the young woman with sign language, I asked her about any unforgiveness she may have had toward her mother. As soon as she was asked that question, she became agitated and responded that yes she had some issues with her mom. We led her through prayers of forgiveness and renouncing the judgments toward her mother. Her countenance noticeably changed after these prayers and ministry.

We then began to pray for her ability to hear and to speak. Within minutes, for the first time in her life, she began to hear and speak simple words! We spoke the name of Jesus softly to her, and she repeated his name; it was the first word she ever spoke. As we continued to pray and work with her, her hearing and speech were functioning very well and her medical doctor was astounded. God is the healer—we simply prayed. God's grace for healing was restricted by the unforgiveness this young woman had toward her mother, and the miracle occurred after she forgave and broke judgments toward her mother.

Choosing to forgive and release anyone who has hurt you, whether real or perceived, is essential for God's grace to flow freely in your life. It might be a parent, or it may be another authority figure, friend, family member, etc. You must forgive others and break agreement with any judgements that you have toward them to live fully in God's grace.

FORGIVENESS AND HONOR ARE CONNECTED

Judy discovered that honor and forgiveness are connected when she was profoundly impacted by a message I gave one Sunday on the importance of honoring our parents. In the message, I explained how honor positions us to live a long and prosperous life (Eph. 6:2-3). However, if you are holding onto judgments toward your parents, even if you say you have forgiven them, then you are dishonoring them. We are to honor our parents irrespective of their behavior—honor releases life. True honor is free of judgments, and genuine forgiveness will free us from the hurts of the past.

The following week, Judy shared with the congregation her testimony of forgiveness after hearing the message. She explained to the church that at the age of four, her father abandoned her mother, brother, and herself—many years would pass before she saw her natural father again. At the age of six, Judy's mother remarried, and her stepfather was an abusive alcoholic, frequently beating her and her brother. When she was ten, her mother remarried again. Sadly, this stepfather sexually molested her for the next seven years. To escape this horrible situation, Judy found the first man who would marry her and left home at the age of seventeen.

At the age of twenty eight, Judy became a Christian and was hungry to grow in her relationship with Jesus. In her words,

> I was serious about serving God. I went to Bible studies, Bible College, conferences, etc. I wanted to forgive everyone, including my mother for the anger, rage, hate, and guilt that had been building in me for years. I had much to learn about forgiveness. By God's grace, over time I could forgive and walk in peace and compassion toward those who hurt me. I chose to forgive—to become better and not bitter—and I wanted freedom through Jesus Christ. I went to every Bible study I could and learned as much as I could as fast as I could. The main faith lesson I learned was that I needed to forgive others, so I worked on forgiveness. Now, it took a while; it took a long while and a lot of prayer, but by God's grace I was able to forgive and walk in peace and compassion.

Judy then shared about another painful incident with the stepfather who had sexually violated her when she was younger. When Judy's daughter was ten years old, her stepfather repeatedly molested her daughter. With regard to the difficult process she went through after discovering that this had been happening to her daughter, she shared,

> So, all the rage, anger, and hate that I once had dwelling inside of me returned with a vengeance—it came flooding back to me like a tsunami wave. Now I'm a Christian,

and you're not supposed to feel that way, right? Well, I did. It was a long hard road once again, but I forgave him and walked in peace and compassion again. So much compassion that I flew from California to New York to see my biological father who I never knew. He was on his deathbed, but God in his grace and mercy allowed me to lead him to Jesus just before he died two days later. Then a few years later, that same grace and glory came, and I was able to lead my stepfather, the man I hated most in this world, to Jesus.

Judy then shared about how the message of honor and its relation to judgments affected her:

Pastor Bob gave a life-changing message on 'Honor' last week; it convicted me as I realized I forgave but did not honor any of my parents. I knew the scripture but justified myself because I felt they did not deserve it. I also acknowledged I had forgiven, yet had judgment toward each of them. This was not God's way. I had to get this righted, right away. I repented for years of sin with God and toward each of them. In the process, I suddenly became aware that this choice of releasing them from judgments was not about them, but about me, and my obedience to the Word of God, which is for my good. Now I am truly a captive set free.

They're all gone now, but I am honoring them despite the pain they caused. I am so happy for that; I am so free now. It was because of this message about honor last week. I did forgive them, but I held them in judgment.

And it wasn't that I couldn't honor them—I thought I couldn't, but it was more that I wouldn't. I justified it, and I think we all can do that. We justify our behavior and our beliefs. We'll even fight to defend our wrong beliefs related to forgiveness.

Judy, like many of us, had read and heard all the teachings of Jesus about forgiveness but was unable to release her parents and stepfather fully from judgments. When she forgave and released them from the judgments, she found freedom and peace unlike that which she had ever known. Judy has passed on, but her testimony of forgiveness and healing continue to help others who have experienced similar situations find freedom from the pain of past hurts and abuse.

PRAYERS OF FORGIVENESS

Perhaps someone has hurt or wronged you deeply. Can you forgive them, and release them from judgments today? To live your life as God intended and fulfill your dreams, you must live in grace and forgiveness toward others. Give the Lord permission to remove judgments in your heart toward those you have struggled forgiving, and to begin the process of healing your heart from the pain you experienced. Here is some language that you can use to help you get started:

Father, I choose to forgive the ones who have hurt me deeply and sinned against me. I forgive ……………... (name). I give them the gift of unconditional forgiveness, with no conditions attached. They owe me nothing. I trust you to turn it for good. Lord, I forgive him/her and ask that you forgive them Lord and forgive me for judging him/her.

Lord, I also forgive myself for my failures and mistakes. I let go of it all. Lord, I want to be free. I want to break the hold of the enemy in my life. I put the cross of Jesus Christ between my heart and everything I was due to reap from the law of sowing and reaping, because I do choose mercy over judgment.

Jesus, I invite you now to go back to the past, where the hurts and wounds have occurred, and begin to heal me of the .... (anger, hate, self-hate, rejection, fear, etc.) that took place.

CHAPTER 7

Worry-Free Living

—〰—

"Throw all your anxiety onto him, because he cares about you."

— *1 Peter 5:7 CEB*

*"Fear and worry are interest paid in advance
on something you may never own."*

—*John L. Mason*

The Effects of Stress and Worry

Worry causes stress and fear. Your body can process small amounts of stress; however, excessive stress—whether real or perceived—can create emotional, mental, and physical problems. Proverbs tells us, "A peaceful heart leads to a healthy body..." (Prov. 14:30 NLT). Conversely, a heart filled with worry and fear can open the door to health issues.

Prolonged stress can deplete your immune system, leading to sickness and disease. Stress can hinder your ability to emotionally process the demands of life, weakening not only your physical body but your cognitive functions as well. Stress can also create unhealthy fear and phobias. Unresolved stress and fear will hinder you from living victoriously.

In her book *Who Switched Off My Brain?*, Dr. Caroline Leaf, a researcher in cognitive neuroscience since 1985, states that 87% of the illnesses plaguing people today are a direct result of their negative thought life. Her research indicates that "toxic emotions can cause migraines, hypertension, strokes, cancer, skin problems, diabetes, infections, and allergies."[1] She concludes that what we think about tangibly affects us both physically and emotionally. Her studies indicate that fear triggers more than 1,400 known physical and chemical responses and activates more than thirty different hormones and neurotransmitters.[2]

Proverbs describes the effects of unresolved anxiety or worry in your life: "Anxiety in the heart of man causes depression, but a good word makes it glad" (Prov. 12:25). *Merriam-Webster Dictionary* defines anxiety as a "painful or apprehensive uneasiness of mind usually over an impending or anticipated ill. A fearful concern or interest. An abnormal and overwhelming sense of apprehension and fear often marked by physiological signs (as sweating, tension, and increased pulse), by doubt concerning the reality and nature of the threat, and by self-doubt about one's capacity to cope with it." Considering the depth of the modern definition of anxiety, it is no surprise the writer of Proverbs long ago indicated that anxiety could lead to depression.

Of course, not all depression is caused by anxiety, worry, and fear. Some forms are a result of physiological and brain chemical disorders. However, many struggle with mild or even severe forms of depression related to the spiritual root causes of worry and anxiety. Allowing worry to rule in your heart can lead to stress, fear, and, as just stated, forms of depression. Remember, you have a choice: trust God or live in worry. For the Christian, worry is a characteristic of unbelief, a manifestation of a lack of faith in God's promises. Persistent anxiety will eventually breed fear.

Did you know that 40% of what you worry about will never happen? Alternatively, are you aware that 30% of what concerns you are things from the past that cannot be changed? Likewise, do you realize that only 10% of what you worry about are considered significant issues? Did you know that 12% are about health-related issues that will never happen?

This means that an overwhelming 92% of what you—and everyone else—spend so much time worrying over will never take place. Based on these percentages, only 8% of worry can be considered legitimate.[3] Regarding these legitimate concerns, we can trust in God's provision for peace and joy during life's challenges. Benjamin Franklin said simply, "Do not anticipate trouble or worry about what may never happen. Keep in the sunlight." This is good advice, as most of what we worry about will never happen.

When worry and fear control you, you rob yourself of the authority God has given you as his child and as a citizen of heaven. In fact, your negative thinking, emotions, and words create ungodly beliefs in the mind which can empower demonic forces against you (2 Cor. 10:4-5). Jesus has stripped the devil of his authority and commissioned you with his authority; however, the enemy can regain power over you through your unbelief. When you agree with the enemy's lies, you relinquish the authority Jesus has entrusted to you and by default, you empower the enemy. Unbelief and fear are contradictory to faith; a counterfeit to what is real.

Learning to live out of your relationship with God and the truth of his Word empowers you to live free of worry and fear.

The prophet Isaiah wrote, "Those with sound thoughts you will keep in peace, in peace because they trust in you" (Isa. 26:3 CEB). Concentrating upon the truth of God's promises will create peace in your life. An abiding relationship with Jesus grows your confidence that God will keep his promises.

Faith operates from a place of trust and rest. If your mind is unrenewed regarding your identity in Christ and God's promises, you will not be at rest in the various circumstances of life. Faith comes from the heart, not the mind, but a renewed mind creates a framework for faith to operate from God's perspective—where nothing is impossible.

Oswald Chambers, an early twentieth-century Christian evangelist, teacher, and author of the devotional *My Utmost for His Highest*, stated regarding our ability to trust God's promises, "Our capacity in spiritual matters is measured by the promises of God. Is God able to fulfill His promises? Our answer depends on the depth of our relationship to God, which will determine our trust in His promises."[4] Your ability to confidently trust God will determine whether you abide in peace or live in worry.

JESUS IS OUR PEACE

The foundation for your peace is found in Jesus—he is your peace. Before his crucifixion, Jesus shared the Passover meal with his twelve disciples. He knew that Judas was about to betray him, and that very soon he would return to his Father. In John 14, Jesus began a discussion with the disciples to prepare them for his departure and to equip them to walk in his peace. In John 14:1, he told them, "Do not let your heart be troubled..." (NASB). The English word "troubled" in this verse is translated from the Greek word *tarassō*, which means "distressed" or "agitated." It can also mean "to cause acute emotional distress or turbulence—to cause great mental distress."[5] The Greek word *tarassō* describes a severe inner distress and agitation, and the root cause of this distress is worry and fear about circumstances. In the case of the disciples in John 14, their agitation stemmed from concern regarding the imminent departure of Jesus. They did not understand that it was better for Jesus to depart from them. Once crucified, resurrected and ascended, Jesus would send the promise of the Father, the precious Holy Spirit to dwell in and with them—and likewise in and with all who believe (John 14:16-18).

Remember the story I told in the last chapter about my stolen van? My anger and anxiety got the best of me and I became extremely distressed and agitated. I was worried sick over the condition of the van and the financial costs, even though I had no control over the situation. My agreement with negativity empowered the enemy to torment me with anger, worry and fear. This created a debilitating emotional and mental state that ultimately prevented me from sharing about the Guatemala mission trip with our church family that Sunday. I allowed myself to be miserable for nearly 48 hours, and my agitation affected not only my family but everyone I encountered. In that situation, I feared the worst rather than trusting God to bring good out of a challenging circumstance. Truly, worry and fear are interest paid in advance on something you may never own.

John Wimber, one of the founders of the Vineyard Church, used to say, "Stay on the rug of peace." Learning to abide in the peace of God is essential to living as an overcomer. God's kingdom is not food or drink, but "righteousness and peace and joy in the Holy Spirit" (Rom. 14:17). Because you are justified and made righteous in Christ, positioned with him in his ascension victory, you are living from heaven toward earth, complete in his peace and joy. Joy and peace are characteristics of your life in the Holy Spirit (Gal. 5:22-23) and should be normal for you as a believer, even during the challenges and problems of life.

Jesus is the way, but the destination is the Father (John 14:6). His ultimate mission is to bring us to the bosom of the Father, and it will be sufficient or enough for us—"Philip said to Him, 'Lord, show us the Father, and it is enough for us'" (John 14:8 NASB). As I discussed in chapter four, the English words "sufficient" or "enough" in this verse derive from the Greek word *arkéō*, meaning to be content or satisfied, filled with unfailing strength. It also means to ward off negative things from the world, such as fear and worry—which are the opposite of faith and peace. The revelation of the Father's love for you will strengthen and sustain you against worry and fear—it is enough. After you gaze upon the face of God, circumstances look different, and you reflect his presence and peace.

In John 14:27, Jesus declared to the disciples, "Peace I leave with you; My [perfect] peace I give to you; not as the world gives do I give to you. Do not let your heart be troubled, nor let it be afraid. [Let My perfect peace calm you in every circumstance and give you courage and strength for every challenge]" (AMPCE). Jesus told the disciples not to worry and assured them that he would take care of them and give them his peace. What happened? They worried and became fearful. We often do the same. Like those first disciples, we allow worry and fear to dominate our thinking and emotions when circumstances seem contrary to God's promises.

The cautions Jesus gave the twelve disciples still hold true for us today. Peace is to be the standard characteristic for the follower of Christ. It has been said that "Fear is False Evidence

Appearing Real—F.E.A.R." Fear is not legitimate for a believer, unless it is the reverential fear of the Lord. Unfortunately, many of us remain tormented by worry and fear instead of abiding in God's peace because of our lack of trust in his promises.

As a believer, you have been united with Christ and adopted into God's family. You are no longer an orphan or a fearful slave, but a beloved child of God, a citizen of his kingdom with all of God's rights and privileges. As Jesus is, so are you now, completely accepted and loved by the Father (1 John 4:17), an heir of God and a joint heir with Christ. The fact that he defeated the powers of darkness and ascended to the throne empowers you to walk in his authority. The basis of your peace is the reality that Jesus has overcome the world. You can live in Christ and his victory, free from fear and worry. Do not allow your present circumstances to rob you of your security in Christ. Jesus is the essence of your existence—your peace flows from him. Your security and success is found in God, and he has empowered you to do the impossible in your generation because he is with you.

PURSUE GOD FIRST

Most of us are aware that God promises in his Word to protect, deliver, and provide for us, but few act in faith upon these promises. During challenging circumstances, many often see God as a distant friend, a harsh judge, or an unloving Father. God is none of these; he is a good Father. Lack of relationship and intimacy with God creates underdeveloped faith and trust. As you spend more time with God through prayer, worship, and his Word, your relationship deepens, faith and trust grow, and worry flees. Learning to trust God and his promises despite present circumstances is vital to remaining in God's peace and overcoming life's challenges.

The book of Hebrews describes entering into the rest of God, which is available to the believer by faith (Heb. 4:9-11). In the Sabbath rest of the Lord, we can cease from weariness and the pain of human labor. What is required to enter this rest? Simple childlike faith and trust (Mark 10:15). A child's faith is simple; a child does not need a detailed plan from his or her parents to believe that everything is going to be okay. Learning to remain in God's love and peace is indicative of childlike faith, but it is also a measure of mature faith. Learning how to stay in a place of peace, amid the storms of life, empowers you to live life worry-free.

One key to remaining in the peace of God is to maintain correct priorities. Focusing on the wrong priorities in life is a primary reason why so many people are consumed with worry and fear. In Matthew 6, Jesus described the benefits of right priorities: [31] "Therefore do not worry, saying, 'What shall we eat?' or 'What shall we drink?' or 'What shall we wear?' [32] For after all these things the Gentiles seek. For your heavenly Father knows that you need all these things. [33] But seek first the kingdom of God and His righteousness, and all these things shall be added to you" (Matt. 6:31-33). Jesus clearly tells us to make the pursuit of God and his kingdom values our primary quest in life, and God will then abundantly provide for our material needs. Simply stated: seek God first, not security or even the answers to your problems. Most people, including Christians, are seeking security in the things of this world rather than in the Creator of this world. Answers to questions and strategies in life are discovered through intimate relationship and friendship with God.

Much of our anxiety and worry in life is caused by planning without God. We look at the natural circumstances we are facing, and apart from a renewed mind that embraces God's perspective, we estimate that there is no hope in our situation. Former slaves do not overcome walled cities. Five loaves and two fish do not feed thousands. With human reasoning, the lost are lost, the sick are sick, and the dead are dead. We look at society and world problems and rationalize that change is impossible; yet renewed perspective understands that it is the power of the Gospel that changes lives, cities, and nations.

Matthew 6:25 (AMPCE) states, "Therefore I tell you, stop being perpetually uneasy [anxious and worried] about your life, what you shall eat *or what you shall drink*; or about your body, what you shall put on. Is not life greater [in quality] than food, and the body [far above and more excellent] than clothing?" Continual anxiousness and worry consume us when we have the wrong set of priorities in life. Real peace and rest comes to those who have fallen in love with Jesus and have allowed the pursuit of him and his kingdom to be their first priority in life.

Learning to remain in God's peace and rest does not mean that you do not go to school, work jobs or establish careers. It means that while pursuing careers, family, and normal life, you are pursuing Jesus and the culture of his kingdom foremost in all that you do. You learn to trust and rest in his promises, nature, and the presence of God while living in an earthly realm. Communing with the Holy Spirit and abiding in his presence releases the very peace and joy of Christ that guards your heart and faith despite the hardships in life. You can endure the storms because the Prince of Peace is with you. He still calms the stormy seas.

The book of Proverbs provides sound advice regarding anxious thoughts: "All the days of the desponding *and* afflicted are made evil [by anxious thoughts and forebodings], but he who has a glad heart has a continual feast [regardless of circumstances]" (Prov. 15:15 AMPCE). Do not muse about forebodings, what could happen or go wrong in the future; they are evil in nature. The writer of Psalms reasserts this truth about worry: "Do not fret—*it* only *causes* harm" (Psalm 37:8b). The enemy wants to bring you into an agreement with fear, keeping you in worry and anxiety instead of the peace and joy of Christ.

CAST YOUR CARE

Peter provides a practical approach to living worry-free. In 1 Peter 5: 7 (CEB), he explained that we should "throw all your anxiety onto him, because he cares about you." The English word "anxiety," translated from *mérimna* in the Greek, denotes distractions, anxieties, burdens, and worries.[6] Peter clearly tells us how we are to deal with each day's worries—throw them all on the Lord who cares for you compassionately.

The English word "throw," or in other translations "cast," is derived from the Greek word *epiriptō* which implies a forceful, even violent approach to dealing with your anxiety and worry. *Epiriptō* refers to throwing, hurling, arising, sending, striking, and driving out—each of these are forceful terms.[7] Peter, being a fisherman, was well acquainted with *epiriptō*. To "throw" or "cast" fishing nets, fishermen had to use forceful effort to place the heavy nets strategically into the water. Your cares and anxiety weigh you down; you must be intentional to throw or place your care on the Lord. The word *epiriptō* also means "to cause responsibility for something to be upon someone— 'to put responsibility on, to make responsible for.'"[8] In other words, Peter is instructing us to put the responsibility of our cares and concerns upon Jesus. Refuse to live under the weight of burdens that were not intended for you, and allow Jesus to help you carry the concerns and worry of this life.

Jesus also said, "[28] 'Come to me, all you who are struggling hard and carrying heavy loads, and I will give you rest. [29] Put on my yoke, and learn from me. I'm gentle and humble. And you will find rest for yourselves. [30] My yoke is easy to bear, and my burden is light'" (Matt. 11:28-30 CEB). In biblical times, teams of oxen plowed fields or pulled carts. One of the oxen was the lead and would help the other ox as they labored together. Jesus, who is the lead person in your union with him, promises to be the partner who will shoulder the load in your journey. In fact, through the journey called life, as you learn to rest in his effort and his grace, you will find rest in your soul. Cooperate with him as he leads!

Honestly, like most people, learning how to throw my cares upon Jesus and allowing him to help with life's heavy burdens has been challenging for me at times. My rational mind, and perhaps yours, has a tough time simply trusting God and resting in him. God knows this, which is why he instructs us to allow our thinking to be transformed in order that we may "see" and "understand" from his perspective (Rom. 12:2). It takes time, but God is patient through the process of changing your reasoning. Learn how to surrender to the Word and Spirit to bring about the changes in your thinking. Living in his peace and rest is priceless—it is worth the time it takes for the Holy Spirit to transform you.

LIVING FREE OF WORRY AND FEAR

One of my favorite books in the New Testament is Paul's letter to the Philippians. It's Paul's joy letter. He uses the words "joy" or "rejoicing" fifteen times in this short book. In chapter four, he develops an understanding of how to pray effectively and abide in God's peace and joy while waiting for answered prayer. Here are some key steps Paul outlines in the book of Philippines to remain in God's peace and joy, free of worry and fear.

1. PRAY WITH THANKSGIVING

The first step to living free of worry and fear is to learn how to pray with thanksgiving from a posture of belief and trust. Paul tells the Philippian believers, "[6] Don't worry about anything; instead, pray about everything. Tell God what you need, and thank him for all he has done. [7] Then you will experience God's peace, which exceeds anything we can understand. His peace will guard your hearts and minds as you live in Christ Jesus" (Phil. 4:6-7 NLT).

Prayer is communion with God. For the Christian, prayer should be as normal as breathing. Your life is in Christ, united together with him, and the Holy Spirit is daily leading and guiding you as you walk with Jesus. Thus, prayer should be normal conversation with your best friend. You rest in him through prayer, releasing worry and receiving his peace.

Prayer promises to bring you into a place of rest and peace. You are to give thanks through the trials, not just when they are over. Your circumstances are not the problem; it is your perception of them that is the problem. How you react will affect whether you abide in his peace and how soon you realize answered prayer. You cannot control the outcome of prayer, but you can control how you respond to the situation as well as how you love others. When you allow worry and fear to consume you, the flow of God's love through you to others is hindered. Each of us should be a representation of God's love, peace and joy to the world.

Prayer with thanksgiving is an expression of confident faith in God. Faith is the assurance that what God promised will be realized, and peace is the fruit of knowing that God has heard and will answer you. Peace is an imparted grace that empowers you to walk confidently through the storms of life, knowing God is in control. It guards your heart against worry and fear.

As his representative here on earth, you are God's delegated authority—your prayers bring the realm of his kingdom to earth. The Church, the followers of Jesus, is called to bring his secrets and his justice to earth. We eagerly anticipate the return of Christ, but the answer to the world's problems is the Church arising into her destiny and calling. A.W. Tozer, a twentieth-century pastor and author wrote, "A scared world needs a fear-less church."[9] When God's people pray from a posture of peace, heaven's authority infuses earth to calm fearful hearts.

Funds Needed!

In the early nineties, Carolyn and I, along with our then-infant daughter Hannah, were on our way to Haiti to serve as missionaries. At that time, and sadly still today, the nation's infrastructure—roads, water, sewer and electric grid—was grossly deficient. Electricity was scarce, sometimes only available for an hour or two a day. Living in Haiti necessitated electrical generators and inverter systems to generate additional electricity to power homes, business, and churches. The small house we were going to rent did not have a generator or electrical inverter system, so we needed to raise funds to purchase one. Just before moving to Haiti, an electrical inverter system became available for $1,500. This amount may seem small, but for a missionary family at that time, it was a significant sum of money. We began to pray and wait expectantly.

One morning a couple of weeks later, I felt led to worship, pray and thank God for the answer to our prayers for the inverter funding. The Holy Spirit reminded me of the promises found in Philippians 4:6-7, and I began to worship and pray with fresh abandonment. A new understanding of prayer came alive in my spirit, that we are to make our needs known to God (who, by the way, already knows all that we need) and thank him in advance for the answer. The Holy Spirit's presence filled my heart, and I was full of his peace and joy.

One of the things I needed to do that day was purchase additional supplies for our move to Haiti. I went shopping and as I was finishing, I ran into a couple from our church at the store. They asked me about our moving preparations and showed excitement for our assignment. A few minutes into the conversation, the wife wrote a check for our mission's work and handed it to me. Without looking at it, I folded the check, placed it in my shirt pocket, and thanked them. We finished our conversation, said our goodbyes, and I finished shopping.

After returning to the apartment and unloading all the supplies, I remembered the check in my pocket. I pulled it out, unfolded it, and to my surprise it was $1,500! I never mentioned our need to the couple, but God knew. The answer came after I deliberately worshiped and thanked God for the provision before there was any sign of it. That day I learned a simple but important truth from Philippians 4:6-7. Prayer—filled with faith and trust that God has heard you, thanking God for the answer that is to come, and resting in his peace through the process of waiting—is powerful and will help you remain in his peace and joy. Since that time, God has asked me to trust him for much larger issues and funding needs. Not all prayer is answered that quickly, nor perhaps in the way that I think it should unfold. However, this simple understanding of how to pray has changed my life, and it will change your life too.

2. REMAIN IN CHRIST

The second step to living free from worry and fear is learning how to remain in Jesus (Phil. 4:7). He is the vine; we are the branches. We are to abide in him just like a branch gleans from a vine or tree. Apart from him we can do nothing and anything less than fully living in Christ is weak faith. Deeper trust develops through spending time with God in worship, prayer and the reading of his word. All fruitfulness in life and ministry flows from your intimacy with God. Learning how to pursue and remain in the presence of God is vital to abiding in his peace.

Jesus is the friend who is closer than a brother, and he said the Father would send the Holy Spirit to be our comforter, helper, and friend. We often make living in Christ complicated, but it is about the value we place on our relationship with him. I will invest my time, energy, and money into what I value—including relationships. I highly value my relationship with Jesus, and love to spend time in his presence; not for what I can just get out of the relationship, but because I love him. Therefore, I spend time with God through worship, prayer, studying his word, and serving others. Do you deeply value your relationship with Jesus, investing your time, energy, and money with God?

The dividend of your invested relationship with God is a mature and confident faith, a faith that is at rest in the circumstances of life. Like any relationship worth investing in, it develops over time and exhibits love, trust, and rest. Ongoing relationship with the Holy Spirit renews your mind to who you are in Christ and the truth of God's promises in his word. From a place of abiding in Christ's love, faith springs from the heart as a passionate response to the lover of your soul. It is not developed through intellectual understanding, but through intimacy as your heart is set ablaze and renewed by God's love for you. Your renewed heart and mind create a place for faith to operate from God's perspective, in which nothing is impossible. This is the faith realm where peace and rest abide, free of worry and fear.

3. Fix Your Thoughts on Things Above

Focus your thoughts on what is true, right, and pure. Paul stated, "[8] And now, dear brothers and sisters, one final thing. Fix your thoughts on what is true, and honorable, and right, and pure, and lovely, and admirable. Think about things that are excellent and worthy of praise. [9] Keep putting into practice all you learned and received from me—everything you heard from me and saw me doing. Then the God of peace will be with you" (Phil. 4:8-9 NLT). In other words, you must refocus your thinking from negativity (worry, fear, etc.) toward positivity (faith, hope, love). We become what we gaze upon. Keep your focus on Jesus, on his nature and character, and you will become more like him and remain in his rest and peace.

Changing the way you think will help maintain both emotional and physical health. Our world is full of negative news and circumstances, but you can refuse to focus on negativity. An unhealthy obsession with what is wrong in your life or the world around you will move you off of the rug of peace. An unrenewed mind will focus on worry—the root is fear. Train your mind to evaluate honestly what you are thinking about. Learn how to identify the fears in your heart that cause worry.

God's word is truth. It guides, it directs, it is a weapon, and it builds your faith. God's word will counter the fear. The Bible is full of God's promises, like blank checks waiting to be written against the bank of heaven. Learn how to focus on the truth of God's promises rather than the negative reports and circumstances that come against you. As you pray and meditate on his word, your faith and confidence in God will grow.

4. Rejoice in the Lord

Lastly, learn to rejoice in God. Paul wrote, "Always be full of joy in the Lord. I say it again—rejoice!" (Phil. 4:4 NLT). Paul told the Philippians to rejoice always because he knew the truth about how powerful joy and rejoicing are for the believer. Joy is not just a characteristic of kingdom life, it is a powerful spiritual force (Rom. 14:17). It was joy that gave Jesus the ability to endure the cross and its suffering for all of humanity (Heb. 12:2).

Joy flows from your relationship with Christ, not from your external circumstances. Joy is an enduring spiritual reality of God's kingdom that will sustain you through challenging times. It is a characteristic entirely different from happiness. While happiness depends on "happenings" and can be fleeting when circumstances change, peace and joy flow from your relationship with God. When you are truly abiding in Christ, his peace and joy remain constant.

Your ability to rejoice in all circumstances will safeguard your faith. God is always good, but suffering is part of your Christian walk. Difficult events happen in life, and many times you have no control over them. However, you do have control over how you react. Remember, God works everything for your good. Maintaining a right perspective on problems and suffering will keep you in a place of peace, full of God's joy despite hardships and setbacks.

Paul modeled the importance of always rejoicing in the Lord, even in difficult circumstances. In Acts 16, we read that Paul and Silas were wrongly imprisoned in Philippi. At midnight, they chose to pray and praise God during this impossible situation. Despite their hardship, their worship and joy in Christ positioned them for a miracle. God suddenly sent an earthquake that shook the prison, broke everyone's chains, and opened the prison doors. They were delivered, and the Philippian jailor and his household came to Jesus that night.

Later, in Paul's letter to the Philippian Christians, he encouraged them to rejoice in Christ. "Whatever happens, my dear brothers and sisters, rejoice in the Lord. I never get tired of telling you these things, and I do it to safeguard your faith" (Phil 3:1 NLT). His words are just as true for us today. Whatever happens, rejoice in the Lord. Never lose your praise and never lose hope. It may be midnight, but God specializes in suddenlies!

Paul learned that he could be content despite circumstances (Phil. 4:11-12) and find real joy by focusing all his attention and energy on knowing Christ (Phil. 3:8) and obeying him (Phil. 3:12-13). Paul learned the truth of Psalm 16:11: "In Your presence is fullness of joy." Real joy is in your union with Jesus—abiding in his presence daily. Remember, your circumstances are not the problem; it is your perception of them that is the problem. Keep your focus on Jesus, and let the joy of the Lord be your strength (Neh. 8:10).

The more you are in love with Jesus, the easier it is to rejoice always. When Jesus is your closest friend, his joy will have no limitations in your life. Genuine faith knows that God holds everything in his hands. You are his beloved, and he has your best interest in mind. A close relationship with Jesus will keep you in his peace, free of worry and fear. Trust him continually and learn to rejoice in him always.

CHAPTER 8

Faith to Realize Dreams

—ʍ—

*"Faith is the substance of things hoped for,
the evidence of things not seen."*

— *HEBREWS 11:1*

*"You will have as much joy and laughter
in life as you have faith in God."*

— *MARTIN LUTHER*

CALCULATING WITH GOD

HAVE YOU EVER CALCULATED WITHOUT God? I have, and most people
I know have too. The disciples did as well. Again, the story of the
loaves and fish provides a great example of this. One day when
Jesus was preaching to a multitude of thousands, they realized it
was getting late and the crowd needed something to eat (Matt.
14:13-21). Jesus told the disciples to feed the people. Perplexed,
they took inventory of their food supplies and found a boy with
five loaves and two fish. Jesus knew exactly what he was about to
do. He was attempting to awaken their faith in a situation that

was beyond their resources. Your resources are not sufficient to accomplish what God has called you to, but Jesus is enough.

The disciples reasoned among themselves, "How are we to feed such a multitude with only a couple of fish and a little bread?" Unbelief sees the lack in every situation. Jesus responded to their negativity by telling them to seat the people in groups of fifty and one hundred. He took the bread and fish, blessed it, and gave the food to the disciples to distribute. The Greek verb used for "gave" is in a form that means "continuing action."[1] In other words, Jesus *kept on* giving food to the disciples and it continued to multiply, feeding nearly 20,000 people. I believe that had the disciples acted in faith on Jesus' word to give them something to eat, God would have worked the miracle through their hands!

God's math operates differently than our math. With God, one person can chase a thousand, but two can chase ten thousand (Deut. 32:30 and Jos. 23:10). That is exponential in nature— a force multiplier, in military terms. God told Gideon to send thousands of warriors home and to defeat an army with only three hundred men. God says, "Give, and it will be given to you..." (Luke 6:38). His ways defy our human reasoning and his ability to force multiply situations is limitless. Jesus wants us to believe that he is enough—period.

IS JESUS ENOUGH?

Has Jesus ever shifted your thinking? God specializes in molding our reasoning to mirror that of heaven—not of earth—if we allow him. While visiting a missionary friend in Guatemala in 1997, Jesus challenged my thinking about his provision. Just a couple of years prior, Carolyn and I had been through a challenging season and returned discouraged from the mission field in Haiti. Life and ministry had not gone the way we planned. At the leading of Jesus, we had walked away from engineering careers and good salaries to serve him in full-time ministry, beginning in Haiti. Yet our time there was consumed with constant prayer and worry about our finances. We had very little resources and struggled to cover expenses—something we had never walked through before as engineers.

One morning during that trip to Guatemala, I went out for a prayer walk and had some concerns to share with Jesus. It was a beautiful Guatemalan morning. The temperature was perfect, the sky was bright blue, and beautiful flowering plants and bushes lined the streets. It was peaceful and serene. Sadly, I wasn't seeing much beauty that day. I was frustrated and stressed over the circumstances that had unfolded in Haiti and then continued after our return to the States. My prayer with the Lord that morning was more complaining with him than communion with him. It went something like this: "Lord, I thought you said we would minister in the nations, helping to train disciples and future leaders of the Church? Why, Lord, were our finances such an issue when we were missionaries in Haiti?" By the way, I was also in denial of any personal responsibility for our situation; I shifted the blame on others and God. When we question God it is often veiled frustration and criticism. Fortunately, he is longsuffering.

Despite my agitation and negative thinking, Jesus began to reveal his thoughts about the situation to me. He gave me a dramatic vision of himself and the world. I saw the Lord, very large and miles high in stature, standing on the earth in North America. He looked relaxed and at peace. He said to me, "Follow me!" He then took three big strides and was across the Atlantic

Ocean, standing in Europe. He moved with another step into Africa, and then with another step into Asia. He then said to me, "Bob, with me, going to the nations is easy. Just follow me, trust, and obey as I lead!" This visionary encounter with the Lord reset my thinking.

After this experience, I began to realize that Jesus is enough. He never asked me to save the world; he simply asked me to follow him. To know and live in Jesus is everything—he is the greatest treasure. He promises to meet every need in life and ministry. When we calculate apart from Jesus, there never is enough. But when you love, trust, and obey Jesus as he leads, you will discover that he is enough—always. Paul could say with certainty regarding Jesus: "But even beyond that, I consider everything a loss in comparison with the superior value of knowing Christ Jesus my Lord. I have lost everything for him, but what I lost I think of as sewer trash, so that I might gain Christ" (Phil. 3:8 CEB).

Provision and answers to prayer may not manifest in the manner or timing that we would like, but Jesus promises to provide for those who love and obey him. You see, Jesus is enough—period. He patiently works with us to transform our thinking so that we understand this truth and reality. His desire is that we would then simply follow and obey him when he leads us to nations or around the corner to pray for a friend or neighbor.

Faith Perceives

We live in a world that is driven by our senses. What we can see, hear, smell, taste and touch are very real to us. However, "sense knowledge" faith denies us the opportunity to allow God to solve the equation—his way. God's ways are simply not our ways; his methods defy logic and reason. When we calculate with Jesus and follow his leading during situations that may be contrary to our natural logic, we are telling him, "I believe and trust you in this." Faith at its base level is simply trusting God. His word says that he honors faith and it pleases him (Heb. 11:6). Faith moves God's heart, causing the release of his grace, which is an empowerment that aids and assists us in our time of need (Heb. 4:16).

Faith is substantive in nature. It sees the promise fulfilled by positioning itself in hope. In other words, it is an expectant anticipation of the reality of the promise before the manifestation appears. It causes us to act upon God's revealed truth with an assurance of the answer. The book of Hebrews says, "Now faith is the assurance [title deed, confirmation] of things hoped for [divinely guaranteed], and the evidence of things not seen [the conviction of their reality—faith comprehends as fact what cannot be experienced by the physical senses]" (Heb. 11:1 AMPCE).

Faith connects us to the blessings of the kingdom of God and is the key that unlocks heaven's resources and realities into your life. It perceives as fact what is not revealed to the natural senses (God's promises, his revealed will) and takes hold of God's promises to make unseen realities available on earth. The eye of faith observes the unseen eternal realm, and faith enables you to know that those unseen realities and fulfilled promises are real, that they have substance now. Your answers are connected to God through his promises in another realm— a heavenly kingdom—where you are seated with Christ. Faith then pulls God's promises and hidden realities into being, and realizes that answers are in motion even before the mountains start to move.

Faith is not optional for the follower of Christ; it is essential. Smith Wigglesworth, a twentieth-century healing evangelist, known for his strong faith in God's promises, said, "God rejoices when we manifest a faith that holds Him to His Word."² While you can position yourself to increase your faith through reading God's Word, worship and prayer, faith is also a gift that God imparts to your heart. Thus faith is both a fruit of the Spirit and a gift from God. It is not just an intellectual understanding of God's promises, but a revelation to our heart by his grace. Dreamers need faith to overcome the roadblocks to their destiny, and those who fulfill their dreams have extraordinary faith.

Genuine Christianity, led by the Holy Spirit, has the potential to transform our minds completely—to have God's perspective and think like heaven. God desires more than just your good behavior, he wants to mature you and his Church into the fullness of Christ, so that you function with a mindset that nothing is impossible with God. Your faith is strengthened as you observe Jesus and understand who you are in him. The same Holy Spirit who raised Jesus from the dead lives and abides in you as a follower of Christ. This reality is why Paul could declare with confidence, "Glory to God, who is able to do far beyond all that we could ask or imagine by his power at work within us" (Eph. 3:20 CEB).

MOUNTAIN-MOVING FAITH

Faith to move mountains begins with believing that God hears your prayers. In Mark 11, Jesus entered Jerusalem the week before his crucifixion, and described to his disciples an important principle about believing prayer and overcoming faith. The day following his triumphal entry into Jerusalem, Jesus saw a fig tree in the distance and walked toward it. As he got close, he saw leaves on it, but no figs. It was not the season for figs, but Jesus nonetheless expected fruit from the tree. Have you ever noticed Jesus' uncanny desire for fruit in your life, irrespective of the season you may be in? Being in season, or always ready, with God demonstrates your maturity and capacity for greater entrusted responsibility.

In response to the fruitlessness of this fig tree, Jesus cursed it, saying, "Let no one eat fruit from you ever again" (Mark 11:14 CEB). The next day, he and the disciples passed by the fig tree again only to find that it had withered and dried up. Peter remembered the prayer and said to Jesus, "Rabbi, look how the fig tree you cursed has dried up" (Mark 11:21 CEB). Jesus responded, "Have faith in God!" and explained the power of faith in prayer: "[23] I assure you that whoever says to this mountain, 'Be lifted up and thrown into the sea'—and doesn't waver but believes that what is said will really happen—it will happen. [24] Therefore I say to you, whatever you pray and ask for, believe that you will receive it, and it will be so for you" (Mark 11:22-24 CEB).

What mountain was Jesus referring to? A mountain, as illustrated by the fig tree, is any difficulty, hindrance, or impossible problem you are facing. Jesus demonstrated that faith provides an entry point for God to move amid impossible situations. When God's faith is released in your heart, your problem becomes smaller, and you discover an assurance of answered prayer. Your prayers for the situation take on new boldness and confidence with God's faith.

However, what is "faith in God"? Jesus is the author and perfecter of your faith (Heb. 12:2) and you can have God's faith as you learn to keep your focus upon Christ. The moment you take your eyes off Jesus, you lose sight of the primary goal of your faith. Faith to move mountains begins and ends with Jesus. He is your goal, your destination and the reason you do what you do. He is your source of life, your greatest joy, and the motivation to ask audacious requests of the Father. Real faith is rooted in the nature and character of God. As you learn to trust Jesus more, his faith will be imparted to you. Faith is to know Jesus well enough to know what he wants to do in any situation.

THE POWER OF FAITH, PRAYER, AND AGREEMENT

I was reminded recently about the power of faith, prayer, and agreement. There are times when you will need someone or others to agree with you in prayer to see the obstacles move in your life. Jesus said in Matt. 18:19 (CEB), "Again I assure you that if two of you agree on earth about anything that you ask, then my Father who is in heaven will do it for you." There is strength in unity and power in agreement. God is a force multiplier.

Remember, God's math is exponential in nature and so is the prayer of agreement. In Luke 10:1, we read that Jesus appointed seventy other disciples (some manuscripts read seventy-two) and sent them out two by two to proclaim the good news of God's kingdom. The Holy Spirit declared in Acts 13:2, "…Now separate to Me Barnabas and Saul for the work to which I have called them." In Acts 3, we read of Peter and John ministering to the lame man, and through the strength of their unified faith, God released a miracle and the lame man could now walk.

A couple of years ago, our church office received a phone call from a man named Paul, on behalf of his friend Anthony. Anthony was in a coma at a local hospital, suffering from a debilitating heart condition. The doctors had tried various medications and procedures, but Anthony was not recovering and was near death's door. The doctors recommended to Anthony's wife that he be sent to hospice, and that she and the family should prepare for his passing.

Paul heard about the healing ministry at our church and decided to call on behalf of his friend. Paul asked our church secretary if there were a couple of men who would come to the hospital to pray for Anthony and to agree with his family for miraculous healing. Carolyn and I asked two men from our church who are involved with our healing room ministry, Sam and Ed, to go to the hospital to pray for Anthony. They brought along another man, Justin, to pray with them as well.

Do you remember the story in the gospels about four men who carried their paralytic friend to Jesus? You can read one account in Mark 2:1-12. The four men heard that Jesus was visiting a man's house in Capernaum, which was probably Simon Peter's home, teaching and ministering to the people. But as they arrived carrying their friend, they saw a large crowd which made it impossible for them to get into the house to lay their friend at the feet of Jesus. So, what did these men do? They tore a hole in the roof to let their friend down so that he could be near Jesus. That's determination. When Jesus saw their faith, he forgave the man of his sin and healed him of his paralysis.

While Anthony remained in a coma, the men from our church joined their faith and prayed for Anthony's "mountain" to be moved. Ed continued to visit Anthony over the next few weeks to pray with him. His vital signs began to improve, and it was no longer necessary for him to be taken to hospice. Anthony eventually awoke from his coma, to the amazement of the doctors and hospital staff! Within weeks, Anthony recovered and was released from the hospital. Even the attending physician said it was a miracle. What looked impossible became probable through united, faith-filled prayer.

Faith can move mountains. Every miracle we observe connects us to the heart of God. Every mountain that's moved reveals both the heart and hand of God. As you seek God's face, his hand is often revealed.

FAITH OR DOUBT

For most people, it is not a lack of faith in the greatness of God that hinders their miracle, but rather doubt in their hearts. Many people just lack faith in God (or a better translation of Mark 11:22 would be the "faith of God") that releases God's power to change situations (see also Gal. 2:20). God delights when you place a demand on his word, when you stand in faith upon what he has promised until you see your situation change.

Dr. Charles S. Price, twentieth-century healing evangelist and author of *The Real Faith for Healing* said, "You can believe a promise, but at the same time not have the faith to appropriate it."[3] Belief is an assurance of the mind; faith is an assurance of the heart. Faith is not intellectual, but spiritual. Faith flourishes primarily in the heart, not in the mind.

Believing can take opposite forms: faith or doubt. Doubt is the opposite of faith. Doubt may tell you that God does not exist, or that he is unloving or uncaring about your need. To have the type of faith that realizes dreams, you need to remove doubt from your heart. I heard Oral Roberts, another twentieth-century healing evangelist known for great faith, once say regarding faith, "Doubt and do without; with faith believe and receive." Living from expectancy opens your heart to increase in faith. Expectancy will position you to receive more from God—including salvation, healing, health, prosperity, peace and joy, to name a few.

By spending time with God, our faith grows through both cultivation and receiving. Paul says you have been united together in Christ (Eph. 2:6), and to be filled with the Spirit (Eph. 5:18) is to be filled with more faith. Through your union with Jesus and your life in the Holy Spirit, you can increase your enjoyment and relationship with God. As your relationship with him deepens, your ability to communicate with God, and he with you, will increase and God will cause your faith to soar to new heights. I find that communing with God through worship, spending time in prayer, and meditating on his word, cultivates the soil of my heart to receive the "new seed" deposited by the Holy Spirit and nurtures the seeds of promise that are already there (Mark 4:20). There are no short cuts—discipline is needed. As you daily spend quality time in God's presence, your heart will not only grow in faith, but you will position yourself to receive more faith.

While we cultivate our faith through relationship with God, faith is also an imparted grace to our hearts by Christ. Paul said in Romans 10:17, "faith comes by hearing, and hearing by *the* word of God (italics added)." God's word to you, which increases understanding and faith, may come through his written word, an impression, thought, vision, or dream. However God communicates to you, faith will grow in your heart as you receive, believe, and act upon what God has revealed. You simply cannot believe without doubt until you "have the faith of God."

SEEING IS BELIEVING

Do you remember the story of the apostle Thomas, otherwise known as "Doubting Thomas"? Jesus had risen from the dead and began to appear in his glorified body to some of the disciples (John 20). They told Thomas, "We have seen the Lord!" Thomas said in response, "Unless I see his nail scares and can touch him I will not believe he is risen from the dead." Thomas, like most of us, wanted to see to believe.

After eight anxious and agonizing days for Thomas (doubt creates anxiety and negativity—it is fear-based instead of faith-based), Jesus appeared to him and the other disciples. The first thing Jesus said to the group was, "Peace to you." Proclaiming peace over those who struggle with doubt and fear provides a foundation for faith to be established. He then said to Thomas, "Put your finger here. Look at my hands. Put your hand into my side. No more disbelief. Believe!" Thomas responded to Jesus, "My Lord and my God!" and Jesus replied, "Do you believe because you see me? Happy are those who don't see and yet believe" (John 20:27-29 CEB). Thomas saw therefore he believed, but Jesus states that you and I are blessed or "happy" when we believe even though we do not see him.

As a follower of Jesus, this must be your position. You may never see Jesus, but you believe his Word and the testimony of others. You know he is alive through your faith and by the Holy Spirit living in you. Through experiencing your new birth in Christ, the Holy Spirit empowers you to have eyes of faith to see. These are not just metaphorical "faith eyes," but the capacity to receive revelation from God that may enable you to see into unseen spiritual realms.

What happened to Thomas after that encounter with Jesus? Church history records that after Thomas moved from doubt to belief, he traveled to southern India and became a powerful messenger of the gospel of the kingdom of God. Many churches in southern India attribute their existence to the missionary work of Thomas.

It is believed that Thomas was martyred on a mountain near the modern-day city of Chennai, India, and I had the privilege of traveling to St. Thomas Mount several years ago. While standing in the church dedicated to Thomas, I realized that, though he was once weak in faith, Thomas was transformed simply through the revelation of Christ. The encounter he had with Jesus by seeing him in his resurrected glory empowered Thomas to live beyond himself and even to die for Jesus. Today, by the indwelling of the Holy Spirit, we too can know Jesus at a level that removes doubt and releases his faith that moves us into destiny.

In Ephesians 1:17-18, Paul prayed for believers to have a spirit of wisdom and revelation, and for the eyes of their hearts to be illuminated about who Christ is and what he has done for them. Have you ever considered that your heart has eyes? When Paul refers to your heart, it is the center of your spiritual being that knows and relates to God. Through faith in Christ, you have now been given spiritual eyes to see—you have the capacity to know Jesus intimately and understand revelation from God. What you experience with your natural senses is real, but the unseen spiritual world around you is just as real; even more than that, it's eternal. What you see with the eyes of your heart should be as real to you as what you see with your natural eyes.

The ancient prophets were often called seers, as they could "see" prophetically into what God was revealing. This practice of seeing or hearing what God is revealing is still available today to those who have trained their spiritual senses to understand the language of the Holy Spirit. You may discover, as I have, that God often communicates through impressions, thoughts, pictures and visions. Tuning your spirit to the "language of the Spirit" and valuing the impressions you receive are required to grow in your ability to see. Learning how God communicates to you is important—it is a practice that develops over time as you walk with God. Faith works through receiving what God is communicating (apprehending what is revealed by God) and being confident it will come to pass.

The apostle Paul was guided daily by the Holy Spirit, and visionary encounters were part of how the Holy Spirit communicated with him. He was given what the Bible calls a "vision in the night" of a man from Macedonia asking him and his team to come and help them. Twice before this occurred, the Holy Spirit stopped Paul and his team from going into other regions (Acts 16:6-10). The vision enabled Paul to see what God was saying, which empowered him to believe God's direction. His faith was strengthened after receiving God's vision; based on the revelation, he was confident about what the Lord wanted him to do.

Understand that, while you may never see Jesus, you believe and, in that way, seeing is believing. I once heard this statement, "if you can see it, you can have it." I have found this to be true with God's revealed will. Visualization is powerful, and God often deposits a gift of faith through what is revealed to you. Once you see or perceive what God desires for you to apprehend, your faith will soar and the realization of the desired outcome is likely.

Real faith is anchored in your new life in Christ and union with him through the Holy Spirit, which empowers you to come with confidence and boldness before God, to ask in faith for the very things you have need of (Heb. 4:16). Faith-filled vision sees Christ and understands who he is and where he sits now. Your prophetic vision of Christ will release all other vision, because he is the author of your faith. It grows your understanding of who you are in him, as you are anchored in your union with Christ, united together with him in his victory and glory. Seeing him as he is allows you to be changed into his image through understanding that as his follower you share his new life and nature

(2 Pet. 1:4). Your revelatory experience in Christ empowers you to live the words he gives you. Vision captivates, empowers, and moves you to action.

I WANT MY BUILDING BUILT!

Remember the story I shared earlier about constructing our new church sanctuary? During a difficult recession and the worst financial crash since the great depression, God instructed us to build a new church sanctuary. When God gave a word that we were to build, saying, "Bob, I want my building built," he also gave a confirming vision with the word, where I saw Jesus building a stone wall. He was wearing a leather apron and appeared rugged and dirty from the demanding work, yet he was happy and determined to finish the task. Jesus was taking stones and securing them onto the wall with mortar. He had all the strings and measuring sticks needed to ensure the wall was straight as he placed the stones in position. Then he paused in his work, turned to me and said, "Bob, I want my building built." That was the end of the vision. I was speechless, but I also knew God was giving a clear directive as to what he wanted—he wanted a new sanctuary building built.

My vision of Jesus constructing the wall and personally hearing him tell me to build his building gave me the confidence to move forward with the project during challenging times. Faith was deposited into my heart; the vision empowered me to see and believe God's promise and to move forward confidently. I needed God's assurance, as later my faith would be severely tested. As I shared earlier, eighteen months after the project started our contractor quit and filed for bankruptcy. I was frustrated and disillusioned, unsure about what to do next. Then I was reminded of something a friend once said to Carolyn and me, "It is in the crucible that God determines if you are useable." We were in a fiery crucible and our faith was being tried and tested by these contrary circumstances.

I drove to my favorite hiking spot, on top of Mt. Lemmon near Tucson, to walk and pray. As I was hiking, I came to an area with a strand of large and beautiful Ponderosa Pines. I stopped to catch my breath and take in the beauty, when suddenly, I saw Jesus in the Pines. My previous vision of Jesus as a stonemason began to unfold once again, and the Lord reminded me, "Bob, I want my building built." As quickly as I saw the Lord and this vision, it was gone, but the impact of this renewed commission and vision shifted my perspective. It was as though I saw this vision for the first time—it was as powerful as when God had first revealed it to me. A peace came over me, and the worry I was feeling about the project lifted. I was once again confident that with his help, we would be able to finish it. More hard work, prayer, and faith were needed, but with renewed vision, the new sanctuary was completed. Seeing is believing but believing must precede seeing.

ALL THINGS ARE POSSIBLE

In Mark 9, Jesus once told a man who wanted healing for his demonized son, "If you can believe, all things are possible to him who believes." The man cried out with tears, saying, "Lord, I believe; help my unbelief!" Jesus healed the boy. The father was grateful, and the crowd was elated about what God had done. However, the disciples were puzzled, as some of them tried to heal the boy earlier to no avail. They asked Jesus in private about why they failed, and he explained to them that in this case, "prayer and fasting were needed" (Mark 9:29).

What was Jesus communicating in this passage? That more effort was needed on their part to release God's grace and power to heal? In one respect, yes; a lifestyle of prayer and fasting will keep you close to the heart of God and sensitive to the Spirit's leading. Faith grows in this realm—the greater our faith, the greater the release of God's power. However, in another respect, the answer is no. The purpose of fasting is not to convince God to answer your prayer; rather, fasting positions your spirit to hear more clearly from God.

A foundational aspect of prayer is a relational connection with God, and I believe Jesus was primarily telling those disciples (and us today) that our life in God is realized through our intimate relationship with him. All fruitfulness in God's kingdom flows from intimacy. God's power is manifested through intimate surrendered hearts who love to be with him.

Earlier in Mark, just before this story, Jesus was on the Mount of Transfiguration, waiting on the Father to hear what he had to say. Your prayer life is more than just bringing your petitions before God—it is your time with him, sitting at his feet, adoring him and waiting for him to communicate to you as well. In this place of fellowship, God imparts strength, revelation and faith. Remember, "faith comes by hearing, and hearing by the word of God" (Rom. 10:17).

All things are possible as you wait in God's presence, listening to God through prayer. Communing with God this way should be a delight for you, not a burden. Like dew upon the grass in the morning, as you wait daily on the Lord, both in time and in faith, his presence refreshes and nourishes you. Greater faith comes through increased intimacy with God, and this comes through a lifestyle of worship, prayer, and meditation on God's word.

FAITH AND PRAYER EMPOWER ABUNDANT LIVING

In the book of Ephesians, Paul prayed that the believers would progress in maturity and fully appreciate the greatness and power of their salvation (Eph. 1:15-23). This power, he assumed, would be demonstrated both in and through them. In other words, he was praying that the Spirit would help them to know God better, to understand their future inheritance, and to demonstrate God's power. One of the primary themes in the book of Ephesians is that the Church should display the present, physical presence of Christ on earth. We—as the Church, the body of Christ—are filled with the Holy Spirit and are assigned to represent Christ by ministering his life, love, and power to those around us. In other words, our calling is to be transformed into his likeness and to represent him.

Paul states in Ephesians 3:20, "Now to Him who is able to do exceedingly abundantly above all that we ask or think, according to the power that works in us." The English word "abundantly" in this verse is translated from the Greek word *hyperekperissoú*, which means: "beyond all measure, superabundant, excessive, overflowing, surplus, over and above, more than enough, extraordinary, above the ordinary, more than sufficient."[4]

Jesus said that He came to give life—not just ordinary existence, but life in fullness, abundance, and prosperity. In John 10:10, Jesus said, "The thief does not come except to steal, and to kill, and to destroy. I have come that they may have life and that they may have it more abundantly." Here the word for "abundantly" is *perissós*, which shares the same root as the Greek word *hyperekperissoú* found in Ephesians 3:20. Jesus said that he came to give life—not just ordinary existence, but life in fullness, abundance, and prosperity, beyond all measure, superabundant! Consider the contrast in John 10:10: the enemy wants to rob and destroy, but God wants you to overflow excessively with his love, grace, and provision. The grace on your life draws upon the inheritance that is already yours in Christ! God releases increased favor to those who pursue his purposes.

Remember, Jesus is the perfect representation of the Father and his nature. God's covenant with you is one of abundant living. To experience true biblical abundance—spirit, soul, and body—you must first believe this is God's highest desire for you. Faith is required. The next step is to surrender yourself completely to Jesus, obey his commands, and follow him. The enemy wants to rob you of your abundance in God and prevent you from fulfilling your God-given purpose and calling. He comes to rob you of God's blessings, to oppress your body through sickness and disease, and to destroy everything you love and hold dear. Faith and obedience are necessary in order to live as an overcomer.

In the Ephesians 3:20 passage, Paul says that God is able to do "above all that we ask or think." Think for a moment about the riches of God's kingdom that are available to you through Christ. Yet what you know, what you have seen, and what you have tasted, is just a fraction of the revelation of God's full glory. In 1 Corinthians 2:9, Paul quotes from Isaiah, "Eye has not seen, nor ear heard, nor have entered into the heart of man the things that God has prepared for those who love Him" (See also Isa. 64:4; 65:17).

Through prayer, you gain divine perspective. Prayer positions you to catch God's revelations and see things from his outlook. You experience and participate—here in the present moment—in your eternal inheritance, and your heart begins to discover the revelation that God can do for you far beyond what you can imagine and that nothing is impossible with him. God longs to work through emptied, yielded vessels who are just in love with Jesus.

The Church has a profound impact on the world because Christ is in her. Jesus said in John 14:12, "Most assuredly, I say to you, he who believes in Me, the works that I do he will do also; and greater works than these he will do, because I go to My Father." How are we to do greater works than him? Through faith and the power of the Holy Spirit working in you. As you discover the One within, the impossible becomes probable. God wants to show himself strong through his Church to preach the gospel to the poor, bring healing to the sick and brokenhearted, deliver the captives, and to demonstrate his love and compassion toward humanity. It does not matter who you are or what you've done; your confidence is in Jesus, and in his power and dominion. As you recognize your authority as a believer and begin to walk in the fullness of Christ, you will impact your world and see dreams fulfilled.

Jesus is the fullness of God and we, the Church, are the fullness of Christ. Jesus is in us, and he is the fullness of every spiritual blessing. All that pertains to life and godliness are found in him. Simply said, Jesus is enough! Paul confirms this in Ephesians 1:22-23 (CEB), "[22] God put everything under Christ's feet and made him head of everything in the church, [23] which is his body. His body, the church, is the fullness of Christ, who fills everything in every way." You are part of Christ's glorious Church who lives from her place of inheritance in him. This truth is the essence of your faith—rooted in Jesus, anchored in his love and victory. Jesus is the author and finisher of your faith!

CHAPTER 9

Prayer that Ends Droughts

—m—

*"The prayer of the righteous person is
powerful in what it can achieve."*

— JAMES 5:16 CEB

*"The church has been negligent of one thing...
She has not prayed the power of God out of heaven."*

— JOHN LAKE

YOU CAN STOP PRAYING NOW ...

I ENJOY READING THE BIBLIOGRAPHIES of great men and women of
God. Their daring exploits are inspiring and faith-building.
Their humanity, struggles, and trials remind me that with God,
all things are possible. Trial and testing occur with every person—no one is immune—including those used significantly by
God. Spiritual maturity develops through absolute dependence
upon the Greater One within. Learning how to abide in God's
presence through prayer and communion is essential to living
from his victory and fulfilling your purpose in life.

Hudson Taylor was such a man. Used by God to blaze a trail for the gospel in China during the nineteenth century, his faith, prayer life, and determination are inspiring. An unknown source tells a fascinating story about Taylor's faith and prayer during his voyage to China on a sailing vessel. As his ship neared the channel between the southern Malay Peninsula and the island of Sumatra, he heard an urgent knock on his stateroom door. Taylor opened his door only to see the captain of the ship. "Mr. Taylor," he said, "we have no wind. We are drifting toward an island where the people are heathen, and I fear they are cannibals." Taylor asked, "What can I do?" The captain responded, "I understand that you believe in God. I want you to pray for the wind." Taylor answered, "Alright, captain, I will, but you must set the sail." The captain exclaimed, "Why that's ridiculous, Mr. Taylor! There is not the slightest breeze. Besides, the sailors will think I'm crazy."

Finally, because of Taylor's insistence, the captain agreed to set the sail. Forty-five minutes later, the captain returned to Taylor's cabin and found the missionary still on his knees. "You can stop praying now, Mr. Taylor," said the captain. "We've got more wind than we know what to do with!"

Hudson Taylor knew the power of prayer. He spent 51 years in China, and founded the organization called China Inland Mission (CIM). Over the years Taylor and CIM have brought 849 missionaries to China, trained 700 Chinese workers, started 125 schools, established 20 mission stations, and led approximately 35,000 people to Christ.[1] To fund this work, they have raised over four million dollars by faith. He was aware that faith to move mountains is developed through a lifestyle of prayer, which is built upon an intimate relationship with God.

To live the extraordinary life Jesus intends you to live, you must become a person of prayer and communion with God. You must set the sail even when no wind is evident. Faith is a prerequisite to answered prayer. Prayer, based upon the promises of God and flowing from a place of intimacy with Jesus, brings the power of heaven to earth. Mountains move. Lives are changed. God is glorified.

PRAYER IS COMMUNION

Through our faith in Christ and new birth by the Holy Spirit, we have restored fellowship with God and one of the joys of any relationship is communication. Jesus modeled a daily prayer life with the Father that demonstrated how simple and meaningful our fellowship with God can be. For Jesus, prayer was more than just bringing requests to the Father; it was conversing with him in two-way dialogue. Prayer is foremost a conversation with God, and through prayer we learn how to abide in God's presence and engage in two-way conversation with him to bring heaven's agenda to earth. God loves to make known what is on his heart. Effective prayer agrees with the revealed will and purpose of God.

The foundation for effective prayer is intimate relationship with Jesus. As you walk faithfully with him, trust and confidence develop. There are no short cuts to a deep relationship with God; you must be intentional about your spiritual growth, as your prayer life springs from this fellowship. The Holy Spirit will help you in this journey, but you must set aside time devoted to cultivating your relationship with Jesus. Learning how to dialogue with God in simple conversation will yield tremendous dividends in your life. From a place of intimate relationship with God, he will show you how and what to pray.

From a place of intimate relationship with God, he will make known how and what to pray for. You pray from heaven's revelation, bringing that reality into earth's realm. Remember, as a believer, your union with Christ positions you in his resurrection authority and power. You are praying from his victory to realize heaven's desire here on earth.

As it is in Heaven

Through God's Word and prayer, you gain perspective and understand his will. Through your divine union with Jesus, you have unhindered access to heaven's promises and provision. Prayer offers the follower of Christ the potential to bring future realities into the present.

So, you might ask, "How do I pray?" In Luke 11:2-4, Jesus gave instructions to the disciples about how to pray, saying, "When you pray, say: Our Father in heaven, Hallowed be Your name. Your kingdom come, Your will be done on earth *as it is in heaven* (Italics added)." *As it is in heaven* is a phrase filled with spiritual truth and reality. When you pray according to the discovered will of God as revealed through his Word and prayer, you are praying from heaven's perspective and this empowers you to pray for God's kingdom to "come on earth, *as it is in heaven*." You are praying the revealed will of God.

Confidence in prayer develops as you learn to pray according to God's promises and revealed will. I have discovered that I am the most faith-filled and confident when I "know" what and how God wants me to pray. As I then pray according to his nature and revealed will, from a heart of love and humility, I have an inner knowing and assurance the answer is on its way.

Prayer from heaven's perspective empowers you to pray for God's kingdom to "come on earth, *as it is in heaven*." God's kingdom, or God's domain and rule, brings his authority and peace to your earthly situations. Your position is with Christ in heavenly realms (Eph. 2:6). His domain is near, and you should expect answers to your prayers and for situations to change. You are not praying to break through to heaven; you can be confident and expectant in God that as you pray according to his revealed will, the answer is on the way. Your prayers are helping to bring the reality of heaven to earth, which is your assignment (Psalm 115:16).

Francis Frangipane, pastor and author, made this statement regarding praying for God's kingdom to come on earth, "We can look at the conditions of the world and faint or look at the possibilities of God and take faith. To bring revival is to pray for the reality of God's kingdom to manifest on earth. Jesus was not offering His disciples a millennial prayer focus, for that rule of God's kingdom is coming whether we want it to or not! No, but Christ calls us to pray for God's kingdom to manifest in our world today." Well stated—prayer establishes the rule of God's kingdom here, now, not just in the future.

In Jeremiah, we read about God's invitation for the Israelites to enter into future hope and promise: "Ask me and I will tell you remarkable secrets you do not know about things to come" (Jer. 33:3 NLT). God knew his future intent for this wayward nation—one filled with hope. He invited them, and encourages you today, to ask for the secrets and mysteries that God alone knows about. He wants to unveil glimpses of the future to you, to empower you to pray effectively, and bring tomorrow's promises into "today" for you. Many promises are "now words" for you. However, faith, prayer, and obedience are required to see promises and dreams become reality.

Paul wrote, "[18] I pray that the eyes of your heart may be enlightened, so that you may know what is the hope of His calling, what are the riches of the glory of His inheritance in the saints, [19] and what is the surpassing greatness of His power toward us who believe. These are in accordance with the working of the strength of His might" (Eph. 1:18-19). As a follower of Christ, the surpassing greatness of God's power accompanies your life. Because you are in Christ, El Shaddai—God Almighty, empowers your prayer life. This power is not human effort, but the inner strength of his might.

Paul wrote many times—in Eph. 1:19, 6:10, Col. 1:11, and 1 Tim. 6:16—of this power. In these verses, the English word "power" is translated from the Greek *krátos*. *Krátos* means "strength, manifested power, and dominion."[2] The word primarily signifies exerted strength and power shown effectively in a governing authority. *Krátos*, as used in these verses, primarily refer to God's kingdom power, dominion, and majesty as demonstrated through the resurrection of Jesus. You are enthroned with Jesus in his *krátos*: his dominion, authority, and resurrection power.

You are located in Christ, with both his life and his power. "Glory to God, who is able to do far beyond all that we could ask or imagine by his power at work within us" (Eph. 3:20 CEB). Where is the power at work? —within you!

Jesus said in the book of John, "³⁸Anyone who believes in me may come and drink! For the Scriptures declare, 'Rivers of living water will flow from his heart.'" ³⁹ (When he said, "living water,",' he was speaking of the Spirit, who would be given to everyone believing in him...)" (John 7:38-39 NLT). Through your union with Jesus, you are in him and the power within you, through the Holy Spirit, is the same power God demonstrated when he raised Jesus out of the grave.

This means that presently, you have resurrection power attached to your prayer life. What does resurrection mean?

It means reviving and raising things which look dead, and even act dead, back to life. God demonstrated this "power toward us who believe" first "in Christ, when he raised him from the dead, and seated him at his right hand in the heavenly places" (Eph. 1:19-20). The power in you is the same power God demonstrated when he raised Jesus out of the grave; it is resurrection power.

DECLARE THE DROUGHT IS OVER!

A few years ago, the state of Arizona was in a terrible drought. For nearly two years, the drought intensified, causing a serious shortage of rain for two summers that would have normally been our rainy seasons. Arizona, and my city of Tucson, needed rain desperately.

During the height of the drought, Carolyn and I decided to escape the summer heat for a day and travel up the Catalina Highway to the top of Mt. Lemmon. Beautiful and majestic, the Catalina Mountains lie to the north of Tucson and rise dramatically above the valley floor. The Catalina Mountain Highway provides a picturesque view for the city's inhabitants and winds its way through nearly thirty miles of switchback roads to the 9,000-foot summit of Mt. Lemmon, which is the highest peak in the Catalina range. From the top of Mt. Lemmon, you can view the eighty square-mile valley and the city of Tucson below.

After spending some time walking the mountain trails, we decided to sit on some large boulders that overlook the city. The rocks are a beautiful place to rest, take in the view, and pray for the city. We have spent the day on Mt. Lemmon many times over the years, often ending our time in prayer for our city as we take in the view. However, this day was different. As we stood there praying, Carolyn said to me, "Bob, I believe the Holy Spirit says to 'declare that the drought is over.'" When she said that, I immediately knew in my heart that this was God's revealed will and that we were to pray in agreement, declaring over our city and state that the drought was over.

It just so happened, as divine coincidences so often do in our life with God, that I was in the middle of a six-week teaching series on prayer at our church entitled *The Elijah Principle*. Using 1 Kings 18 and James 5:16 passages about Elijah as examples of effective prayer, I was teaching our church body that we should expect our prayers to be effective and powerful when we pray according to God's revealed will.

Carolyn and I prayed and declared for a few minutes that the drought was over for the state of Arizona and the city of Tucson. We called forth rain, declaring clouds to form and for an abundance of rain to fall. At the time, the sky was bright blue with no clouds. Yet we had that sense that something was about to happen. Faith sees as reality what is unseen to natural sight.

The following Sunday, I continued my teaching series and shared with the congregation about how we prayed and declared the "drought was over" from the top of Mt. Lemmon. We encouraged the church to pray in the same manner. I found out a couple of days later that on that same Sunday, a pastor in Phoenix also taught from the 1 Kings 18 passage. Someone suggested that I listen to his sermon and I was surprised to hear the parallels in our messages, including his declaration over Arizona, "The drought is over." God was moving.

Within the next few days, we received that summer's first substantial rain in Arizona. The remnants of a hurricane, which had become a tropical disturbance, made its way across Mexico and eventually impacted Tucson and Arizona with significant rainfall—record breaking in some areas! We rejoiced, thanked God, and kept declaring, "The drought is over!" Ten days later, a second tropical disturbance came through southern Arizona—more record rainfall—and the rain deficit for the entire year of 2014 in Tucson was eliminated with these two storms. Presently, Arizona, like many western states, is still in a drought, but in 2014 we observed the power of united prayer that brought drought-ending rain that year.

THRUST ONTO THE SCENE

Every aspect of God's kingdom manifested here on earth—in people, churches, and life—is first conceived and then birthed by prayer. As described in 1 Kings 18:41-46, Elijah exemplified this truth when, as directed by the Lord, he continued to pray until the promise was fulfilled and rain covered the drought-stricken land of Israel. Effective prayer acts upon the Father's revealed will and intercedes until the promise manifests on earth.

Elijah is an interesting Old Testament character. Revered in scripture and Jewish tradition as a great prophet, God sent Elijah to turn the nation of Israel's heart back to the true worship of Yahweh. Yet we know little about him other than the fact that he was from Tishbe in Gilead. Elijah just appears suddenly in the narrative of 1 Kings 17, bursting on the national scene of Israel in dramatic fashion: "Now Elijah, who was from Tishbe in Gilead, told King Ahab, 'As surely as the LORD, the God of Israel, lives—the God I serve—there will be no dew or rain during the next few years until I give the word!'" (1 Kings 17:1 NLT). God backed the word he gave through Elijah, and a severe drought affected Israel.

During that time, God's covenant with Israel had been violated by their apostacy. Under the perverse leadership of King Ahab and his wife Jezebel, instead of worshipping the one true God of Israel, Baal was worshiped throughout the northern kingdom as the god of rain and fertility, the one who controlled the seasons, the crops, and the land. The writer of Kings declared the severity of the situation due to Ahab's leadership: "...Ahab did more to provoke the LORD God of Israel to anger than all the kings of Israel who were before him" (1 Kings 16:33).

Elijah confronted Ahab, the false prophets, and an apostate nation. God sent fire and rain to confirm that he is God and that Elijah was his spokesperson. The heavens opened and a national revival was underway. Almost overnight, Elijah went from obscurity to notoriety as a great prophet in Israel.

Later, God escorted Elijah from earth to heaven in a flaming chariot (2 Kings 2:11), but his influence was not over, and his name is mentioned many times in scripture, even throughout the New Testament. When John the Baptist began his ministry as the prophetic forerunner to Jesus, people asked him, "Are you Elijah?" and he answered, "No" (John 1:21). Jesus said regarding John, "And if you are willing to receive it, he is Elijah who is to come" (Matt. 11:14). Later, Moses and Elijah appear on the Mount of Transfiguration to talk with Jesus before his crucifixion and redemption of humanity (Matt. 17:1-13).

Elijah, as a renowned prophet in both Jewish and Christian tradition, continues to hold a special place within these communities and in the heart of God. His relationship with God and his earnest prayer for rain (1 Kings 18: 41-45) provide key principles for effective prayer—the type of prayer that ends droughts.

THE ELIJAH PRINCIPLE

In his letter to the twelve tribes dispersed through the Greco-Roman world, James used Elijah as an example for righteous living and faith-filled prayer. James, the half-brother of Jesus, was the first century apostolic leader of the church in Jerusalem, and Church tradition attributes his namesake epistle to him. His letter provides practical instruction to believers about how to live virtuously and victoriously.

An interesting side note is that James was an unbeliever during the earthly ministry of Jesus. However, according to Paul in 1 Corinthians 15:7, Jesus appeared to James after the resurrection and this most likely led to his conversion. The radiance of Christ softens even the hardened hearts of the biggest skeptics. Never quit praying for your family and friends, because Jesus loves them!

James stated in his epistle that righteous living and earnestness in prayer are keys to an effective prayer life: "[16] The earnest prayer of a righteous person has great power and produces wonderful results. [17] Elijah was as human as we are, and yet when he prayed earnestly that no rain would fall, none fell for three and a half years! [8] Then, when he prayed again, the sky sent down rain, and the earth began to yield its crops" (James 5:16-18 NLT). The English word "earnest," or "effective," is translated from the Greek word *energéō*. The word denotes the idea to "act" or to "work."[3] However, it is not primarily human effort—it is spiritual. In this sense, the implication is that God's Spirit is at work or acting on our behalf. The Amplified version of James 5:16b reads, "The earnest (heartfelt, continued) prayer of a righteous man makes tremendous power available [dynamic in its working]" (AMPCE). The basic idea in the Greek is that prayer has energy.

This energy, or power, is available to and through the followers of Christ by the Holy Spirit (Eph. 3:20; Jam. 5:16b). Your prayers, energized by the Spirit, are at work and causing things to change and manifest.

Notice how James compared Elijah to the ordinary reader of his letter in verse 17: "Elijah was as human as we are..." Remember, Elijah was revered as a great prophet in Israel, and early Jewish and non-Jewish readers alike would have known, with little introduction, who Elijah was. James was stating a profound truth that Elijah had a human nature, just like each of us; yet his prayer was effective because he was righteous, and he prayed sincerely. James did not say, "Elijah, the great prophet, prayed and look at the results." Rather, he said (my paraphrase), "Elijah, an ordinary person, like you and me, lived righteously and prayed with faith and zeal. God answered his prayers, and he will answer your prayers too." In this pastoral letter, James was making a point to the believers at that time, and to us today, that we can be effective in prayer like Elijah if we operate in similar prayer principles.

ELIJAH'S PRAYER PRINCIPLES

First, let me define *The Elijah Principle*: "Earnest, sincere prayer by the righteous person, based upon the revealed will of God, when prayed with faith and expectation, is effective and powerful through the resurrection power of Christ and the Holy Spirit."

Elijah received a word from the Lord: "And it came to pass after many days that the word of the LORD came to Elijah, in the third year, saying, 'Go, present yourself to Ahab, and I will send rain on the earth'" (1 Kings 18:1). God revealed his will to Elijah, essentially telling him that he was going to send rain after Elijah confronted Ahab. Elijah was obedient to God's directive and confronted Ahab and the prophets of Baal. God backed his prophet with fire from heaven upon the sacrifice, and all the people fell on their faces exclaiming, "The Lord, He is God!" (1 Kings 18:38-39). The false prophets were executed, and Elijah proclaimed to Ahab that he heard "the sound of abundance of rain" (1 Kings 18:41).

After Israel's heart was turned back to God, the narrative continues with Elijah praying for rain (1 Kings 18:42-46). He was confident in what God had revealed, prophetically hearing the sound of rain before a cloud was in the sky and proceeded to pray until the clouds formed, and the rain fell. I would say this is effective prayer.

Circumstances are subject to change when you operate according to God's revealed will and principles. God is sovereign, and he often acts apart from our involvement. Yet, even though he does not need to, God frequently chooses to partner with us to bring about his purposes on the earth. It is a mystery—God, the Creator, chooses to involve us in his purposes and the advancement of his kingdom.

To fulfill your dreams, it is essential to learn how to work with God as he leads through prayer. Prayer has the power to transform circumstances for you and others. You might be just a prayer away from a dream becoming reality, a promise being fulfilled, or a miracle being performed. Let us look closely at the prayer strategy of Elijah (1 Kings 18:42-46) which made his prayer effective and ended the drought.

1. Righteousness
Elijah prayed as a man in right relationship to God. Elijah, who was a human just like you and me, was prone to weakness,

discouragement, failure, temptation, and sin. However, James stated that Elijah was righteous and that the "prayers of a righteous person are effective." Does this mean that everything Elijah did was perfect and without fault? No, he was a human just like us—this is the point James was making. He made mistakes and was not without sin. However, Elijah endeavored to walk faithfully with God, and God answered his prayers.

You might be wondering, "How righteous do I have to be to pray effectively like Elijah?" Paul wrote in 1 Corinthians 1:30 that "Christ made us right with God; he made us pure and holy, and he freed us from sin" (NLT). Jesus has become your righteousness, holiness, and sanctification. This means that God sees you presently as pure and holy and in right standing with him through Jesus. You are an adopted son or daughter, united with Christ and his holiness, and because of that you pray in right relationship with God. You can approach his presence free of shame and condemnation, knowing that the Father's heart is for you, not against you.

However, while you are righteous through the blood of Christ, scripture also exhorts you to live a holy life and to pursue righteous living (2 Cor. 7:1). Pursuing a blameless lifestyle removes potential hindrances to prayer. For example, Peter exhorted husbands to love and respect their wives: "Treat her as you should so your prayers will not be hindered" (1 Pet. 3:7 NLT). The writer of Psalms stated, "If I regard wickedness in my heart, the Lord will not hear" (Psalm 66:18 NASB; see also Prov. 6:16-19). The Bible states the necessity of living righteously to ensure that our prayers are unhindered and effective.

In other words, you are righteous, but you must pursue a righteous life. If you fall short in any area of your life, be quick to repent (change your thinking, which will change your behavior), ask God for forgiveness, and expect his cleansing (1 John 1:9). You are righteous through what Christ has done—now, live in his righteousness. Allow the Holy Spirit to make you more Christ-like daily (Rom. 8:29).

Elijah had a human nature like us, but he learned to live in right relationship with God. Half-hearted obedience and living produces weak prayer. It causes you to lose confidence and it robs your faith. Further, you hinder the power of the Holy Spirit in your life. God grants grace to the humble, not the proud. You can expect answers to your prayers if you are living a life that is committed and obedient to God, like Elijah. If you are not wavering between two positions and are living righteously in your generation, God will answer your sincere prayers in his manner and timing.

2. CONFIDENCE IN THE WILL OF GOD

Elijah prayed according to the will of God (1 Kings 18:1). God's word revealed his will to Elijah: God promised him that after he confronted Ahab, he would send the rain. Elijah could therefore confidently obey the directive and pray in faith, knowing that he was praying the revealed will of God. God keeps his promises—this is a major part of his unchallengeable nature. He is not fickle or moody, and he never lies. He watches over his word to perform it. His word is his bond.

How do you know what to pray for? This may seem cliché, but you know by hearing what God is saying. Faith is a revelation to the heart, which begins with a word from God. The more your prayers are specific according to the revealed will of God, the more effective they will be. God does not answer vague prayers—pray with specificity.

Some of you may doubt your ability to hear God's voice. Jesus said, "²⁷ My sheep hear My voice, and I know them, and they follow Me" (John 10:27). As a follower of Christ, you are part of God's sheepfold, and Jesus says plainly that you can hear his voice. God may speak through the scriptures, through impressions, through the voice of the Spirit, through pictures and visions, through circumstances, and through other people. Learn to be sensitive and aware of his presence while you are in worship, prayer, and reading his Word. A verse may seem highlighted to you. You may get a strong impression about something or a mental picture. Someone may approach you and say something that seems odd but confirming.

As I shared previously, there is a unique language in the Spirit by which God communicates to each of us. While God's language with all of us may have shared characteristics, you must learn to recognize how God communicates particularly with you. If you are new to communing with God, be confident that you too can "hear" God's voice and know his will in order to pray more effectively. As you pursue God, you will grow in your ability to discern his voice. Remember, any revelation, dream, or vision should agree with the tenor of scripture and the character of God.

The Bible is also full of promises that reveal God's will—in fact, there are nearly 7,500 of them. Learning what promises are applicable for you today is important. Recognize that not all these promises are universal, as some are (were) for unique situations and person(s) at a specific time. An example of a non-universal promise would be God's instruction to Joshua to take the city of Jericho (Jos. 6:3-5)—it was a specific promise to Joshua and the children of Israel.

In Philippians 4, Paul gives an unconditional universal promise regarding provision: "My God will meet your every need out of his riches in the glory that is found in Christ Jesus" (Phil. 4:19 CEB). Unlike the promise to Joshua, the Philippian promise is applicable for us today—it is a universal promise. You should memorize this one—God will meet your every need!

Another consideration regarding universal promises is that some are conditional, while others are not. For example, a conditional universal promise would be 1 John 1:9 which begins with, "If we confess our sins *(conditional)*." Matthew 21:22 says, "And whatever things you ask in prayer, believing *(conditional)*, you will receive," and Psalm 66:18: "If I regard iniquity in my heart *(conditional)*, the Lord will not hear." Unconditional universal promises would be, for example, Psalm 119:105 which says, "Your Word is a lamp for my feet." This is always true, no matter what. Similarly, Titus 2:11 says that God's grace always offers salvation to everyone, which is also unconditional. Finally, Philippians 4:19, as I mentioned in the previous paragraph, would also be another example of an unconditional universal promise. Learning God's revealed will through the universal promises in scripture, both conditional and unconditional, are foundational for establishing a powerful prayer life.

In all effective prayer, the decisive issue is to know God's will, which will give you faith to believe for it. If you are not sure of God's will, however, your prayers will waver and be ineffective. James says, "⁶Whoever asks shouldn't hesitate. They should ask in faith, without doubting. Whoever doubts is like the surf of the sea, tossed and turned by the wind. ⁷People like that should never imagine that they will receive anything from the Lord" (Jam. 1:6-7 CEB). Sometimes our prayers are misguided, filled with soulish desires, and not from the Spirit. Greater clarity about the will of God creates greater faith for answered prayer.

Confidence in prayer develops as you learn to pray according to God's promises and revealed will. John wrote of this truth, "[14] This is the confidence that we have in our relationship with God: If we ask for anything in agreement with his will, he listens to us. [15] If we know that he listens to whatever we ask, we know that we have received what we asked from him" (1 John 5:14-15 CEB). John's emphasis in this passage centers on the confidence we can have from knowing God's will. Notice that John states that confidence begins with our relationship with God. Remember, prayer is foremost a dialogue with God—not just bringing petitions to him. God desires relationship with you. Seek him first, not the answers to your problems. If you only seek answers, often you will not find them; but if you seek God foremost, the answers will find you.

Provided that you are praying in full accordance with God's will, you can be confident that you have what you prayed for. The use of the present tense "we have" in 1 John 5:15 does not necessarily indicate an immediate manifestation of the thing you prayed for, but it does indicate an immediate assurance that the thing is already granted to you by God. It may take a while for its actual manifestation, but time cannot affect this initial assurance. Now, you can pray through the process until the desired result manifests. I have discovered that I am the most faith-filled and confident when I know what and how God wants me to pray for a particular situation. As I then pray according to his nature and revealed will, from a heart of love and humility, I have an inner knowing and assurance that the answer is on its way.

This agrees with the teaching of Mark 11:24: "Therefore I say to you, whatever you pray and ask for, believe that you will receive it, and it will be so for you" (CEB). A more correct translation would be that we have "already received" it. In the same way, 1 John 5:14-15 could be summed up as: "If you know that you are praying for anything according to God's will, you know that he hears you. If you know God hears you, you know that you have the thing you prayed for (this does not necessarily indicate immediate fulfillment)." From a faith perspective, receiving comes at the very moment of praying. After that, the actual manifestation of that which you have already received follows later in God's timing.

How long do you pray? You continue to pray through an issue or for your answer until you see one of three things happen: the manifestation of the answer to prayer, a sense of release by the Spirit to discontinue prayer, or your spirit begins to "praise through." Sometimes the Spirit will lead you to give God thanks and praise for the answer, even though it has not yet manifested. I shared earlier in the book that we praised God for providing us with the $1,500 needed for the electrical inverter system in Haiti, even before we saw any money come in. I heard a worship leader once say, "Sometimes you just need to get your praise on!" How true this is.

God's promises reveal what his will is, but prayer brings the fulfillment of what God has promised. Elijah prayed with zeal and confidence because he had a clear revelation of the will of God. The greater understanding you have about the will of God, the more effective your prayers will be.

3. PERSISTENCE

Because he knew God's will, Elijah prayed with persistence. Bowed down with his face between his knees, reminiscent of an ancient eastern birthing position, Elijah persisted in prayer until clouds formed and rain fell. To persist in prayer requires humility, obedience, and faith in the revealed will of God. Achieving persistence in prayer comes through the confidence you find in understanding you are praying as a righteous person, according to the will of God, and have already received (through the eye of faith) the thing desired.

Elijah persisted in prayer seven times before the cloud formed and the rain began. What if he had quit praying after just six prayer attempts? There may have been no miracle, and history might have been different. He had to persist in prayer until the Spirit gave him a sense of release. It is easy to give up on dreams, promises, and miracles. Like a slow leak, our faith can ebb from us over time, leading us to lose faith, hope, and often quit praying. Jesus said, "Men always ought to pray and not lose heart" (Luke 18:1).

Keep in mind that miracles are the result of prayers prayed either by you or for you. I have wondered what types of prayers were prayed over our church property in the 1950's. Is it possible that some of what we are experiencing today is a result of another generation's prayers? Absolutely. Persistence is a key to realizing the fulfillment of prayer.

In Mark Batterson's *The Circle Maker*, he described a study that investigated the results of motivation and persistence among students. Researchers asked Japanese and American first graders to take a standardized math test. They were not really interested in whether they would solve the puzzle, but in how long the children would persist before giving up. The researchers discovered that the American children lasted an average of 9.47 minutes, while the Japanese children would continue for 13.93 minutes, which was a 40% difference.[4] In the end, the Japanese students consistently scored higher than their American counterparts on the test, indicating more determination and persistence with the Japanese students. Persistence is not only a vital component to solving math problems, but any type of problem we may face. Success in life is often a derivative of persistence in whatever the pursuit may be, including prayer.

Calvin Coolidge, the 30th President of the United States, once said, "Nothing in this world can take the place of persistence. Talent will not; nothing is more common than unsuccessful people with talent. Genius will not; unrewarded genius is almost a proverb. Education will not; the world is full of educated derelicts. Persistence and determination alone are omnipotent. The slogan 'Press On' has solved and always will solve the problems of the human race."[5] God created humanity to persist. We discover who we are and how great God is during adversity. Your obstacle is an opportunity.

Paul wrote to the church in Galatia, "My little children, for whom I labor in birth again until Christ is formed in you" (Gal. 4:19). The metaphor Paul used here indicates a persistence in prayer—like a woman giving birth—that continued until the nature of Christ was formed in them. The persistence Paul described is similar to Elijah's prayer for rain.

Winston Churchill once said, "The nose of a bulldog is slanted backwards so he can continue to breathe without letting go!" That is what persistence looks like. Prayer that takes hold of God's revealed will by faith remains determined until the answer comes. God is bigger than your biggest problem or biggest dream. Do not bring God down to your level of understanding. Rather, pray from his eternal perspective and maintain a "high view," not a "low view" of God. One of the reasons many give up too soon in prayer is that they make a wrong assumption—the answer has not come, so we must have failed. In truth, we only fail when we quit praying. Our reach must be bigger than our ability to grasp.

What do you do when others have their prayers answered, but yours seem to go unanswered? Do not let offense toward God take root in your heart. Focus on what God is doing and persist in prayer. Many of your prayers will take time to material- ize, and some of your prayers will seemingly go unanswered until the day when they are fulfilled. Keep in mind that when God seems to be saying "no," it may merely be a "not yet." His timing is always best.

George Muller, a nineteenth century minister who cared for over ten thousand orphans in his lifetime and relied solely upon God through prayer for provision, recorded in his journal that he prayed for five of his friends to accept Christ. After many months, one of them came to the Lord. Ten years later, two oth- ers were converted. Twenty-five years passed before the fourth man was saved. Muller persevered in prayer for his fifth friend for fifty-two years, until the time of his death. He never gave up believing that his friend would accept Jesus. After Muller's funeral, his last friend came to Christ. God rewarded his faith and persistence—but Muller did not see the full answer to his prayer on this side of eternity.

Jesus told an interesting parable in Luke 11:5-8 about prayer and persistence. A man knocked on his neighbor's door at mid- night to borrow some bread. At first, he was told to go away: "I am in bed and so is all the family." However, the man kept on knocking, until most likely everyone in the house was awake, including the animals. Because he continued knocking, the man opened the door and gave him the bread. Jesus said that the reason he got up and opened the door was not because it was culturally the right thing to do, but because of his neighbor's persistence. The Greek word used here for persistence, *anaideia*, is a very strong one and means "shameless persistence"—a determination that will not take no for an answer.[6]

This parable is found in the first part of Luke 11, which is all about prayer. The disciples have asked Jesus to teach them how to pray, and he gave them what we call the Lord's Prayer as a model. Right after Jesus gave them a model for prayer, he described this parable of the shamelessly persistent neighbor wanting bread. Jesus then gave them a threefold admonition: [9] "And so I tell you, keep on asking, and you will receive what you ask for. Keep on seeking, and you will find. Keep on knocking, and the door will be opened to you. [10] For everyone who asks, receives. Everyone who seeks, finds. And to everyone who knocks, the door will be opened" (Luke 11:9-10 NLT).

A mysterious theme regarding persistence runs through Scripture. It seems God requires persistence in prayer, that we desire something with all our heart and soul and do not give up asking. We read in Genesis 32 that Jacob wrestled with an angel—many scholars believe that this was God himself, a theophany. Jacob wrestled with him all night, and even though in the process his hip was put out of joint as he wrestled, Jacob said, "I will not let you go unless you bless me." He would not let go of God until God blessed him—a shameless persistence. God honored this and blessed him.

In Mark 7:24-30, a Gentile woman begged Jesus to cast a demon out of her daughter. "No," Jesus said, "it is not fair to take the children's food and throw it to the dogs." Yet despite the insult, she would not let him go. She replied, "Even the dogs under the table eat the children's crumbs." Jesus, moved by her faith and persistence, cured her daughter and exclaimed, "Good answer! Now go home, for the demon has left your daughter" (Mark 7:29 NLT).

Earlier I mentioned the story from Mark 2 about four men who carried their paralyzed friend to Jesus. The crowd was so dense that they could not get near him, no matter how much they tried. Desperate for a miracle, they removed the roof of the house and let down the man to Jesus—that is persistence! Jesus healed their friend and he walked home.

One of the ways persistence manifests is in your ability to wait upon the Lord. Isaiah describes a persistent waiting: "[31] Yet those who wait for the LORD will gain new strength..." (Isa. 40:31NASB). I believe Elijah could pray with energy and persistence because he knew what God's will was and he learned how to abide in God through prayer. In chapter eleven, I discuss waiting on the Lord in greater detail.

Persistent prayer is not about knocking on the door of God's heart so much that in the end he eventually answers your prayer. Rather, persistent prayer reflects a deep desire, passion, and confidence in God, and this is why it's so honored throughout the Bible. This type of prayer often comes from a place of great love for God and desire for others to know him.

4. FAITH

Faith is important as you pray. Faith is an assurance that God has answered your prayer. Realize that Elijah believed his prayer was answered even before the answer came (vs. 44-45). God revealed his will to him (1 Kings 18:1) and Elijah obeyed by going to meet Ahab—that is faith. Elijah could pray confidently, with energy and persistence, because he had faith for the miracle (see also 1 John 5:14-15). Elijah had the assurance that he had rain.

Faith is substantive; it is the assurance of the answer even while it is not yet fully in sight. When the eyes of your heart believe God's will for a situation, you have the reality of the answer even though it has not yet manifested. You persist, even if it seems like God is distant, because you know the Lord hears. Psalm 34:7 states, "The righteous cry out, and the Lord hears." You pray from your identity as a rightly related child of God, accepted and heard by your loving Father.

In the parable of the unjust judge and the widow (Luke 18:1-8), God promised to answer quickly, but then Jesus asked this question: "Nevertheless, when the Son of Man comes, will He really find faith on the earth?" We are to pray in faith, knowing God is just. Jesus emphasized the importance of having faith that perseveres. Faith and persistence, based upon the revealed will of God, should characterize your prayers.

We persist and do not give up because we are children of a just God. We pray in faith, believing that "God exists and that he rewards those who sincerely seek him" (Heb.11:6 NLT). If faith fails, then prayer stops. Who continues to pray when they lose faith? Faith releases prayer, and the release of prayer strengthens our faith. If I want more faith, I must look to Jesus, who is the author and finisher of my faith. Faith provides eyes to the heart to see what God is offering.

Faith lives from the revealed will of God. It operates from the invisible realm to the visible realm. Faith is not a condition of the mind, but a divinely imparted grace to the heart. He gives each one of us a measure of faith (Rom. 12:3). Faith comes from God; as you learn to wait on him, he deposits more faith in your heart. Great faith is rarely developed in a moment, though it is a gift from God. Rather, as you walk faithfully with God, your faith also grows as you obey him and exercise the measure of faith he has already given you.

Faith understands God's authority and the power of his promises. The Roman Centurion in Matthew 8 exhibited this type of faith when requesting that Jesus would heal his servant by simply speaking a word. Jesus responded by marveling at the man's faith, and he "said to those who followed, 'Assuredly, I say to you, I have not found such great faith, not even in Israel!'" (Matt. 8:10). Faith, from the Greek *pístis*, is a forward-leaning assurance of the answer because of confidence in the one who's granting the desired petition.[7]

Faith is not an intellectual understanding, but rather it springs from a revelation in your heart by the grace of God. As such, it is an imparted grace given to you by Christ. Whether it is a promise from God's word, or an inspired word from the Spirit, faith builds because of the word illuminated to you. I once heard it said, "Well-developed faith is often tied to well-developed prayers." Prayer, combined with strong faith, pulls the unseen reality of God's promises into our world.

Jesus only did what he saw the Father do (John 5:14). Everything that Jesus did, including putting mud on the blind man's eye, was rooted in his ability to discern and know the Father's will. His discernment enabled him to see and to understand the revealed will of God. Your new life in Christ empowers you to see with spiritual eyes God's purposes.

Perhaps it seems like the heavens are brass and God is distant. During those times, remember to pray from a place of sonship, knowing your identity is as a child of God, related to a loving Father who knows your every need before you ask or think of it. You pray knowing that your identity is in Christ. You pray from a place of trust in the finished work of Jesus. You pray knowing that God's Spirit indwells you, and that your prayers are more than mere human words.

Prayers are like prophecies, with the power to transform the direction of your life. Your prayers have creative power within them. Job says, "Declare a thing and it shall be established" (Job 22:28). Prayers of faith and the decrees of heaven have the power to move mountains before you. Learn to release on earth *as it is in heaven.* George Muller said regarding faith, "Faith does not operate in the realm of the possible. There is no glory for God in that which is humanly possible. Faith begins where man's power ends."

Faith is an expectant anticipation of a promised outcome. Do not despise the day of small beginnings. At first, Elijah only saw a small cloud in the distance before it grew into massive rain clouds. James wrote, "In the same way, faith is dead when it doesn't result in faithful activity" (Jam. 2:17 CEB). Elijah could pray confidently for a miracle because he had faith in the one making the promise. Are you in a challenging situation currently? Can you stand confidently upon what God has promised?

NORMAL PEOPLE, FULL OF FAITH, IMPACT NATIONS
With the eyes of faith, Elijah was assured of what God was about to do, and his faith led him to act. Several years ago, one afternoon while I was preparing for an evening service on a mission

trip to Brazil, God spoke a very poignant word to me. I was preparing to lead a team to minister at a church that night and we
were expecting that God would pour out his Spirit to touch and
heal the people. God said to me, "If you see yourself as merely
human, you will function as merely human. However, if you see
yourself as a supernatural being, empowered by my Spirit, then
you will function as a supernatural being." This word impacted
me. I had fresh confidence that God would work through the
team and me.

It was a powerful meeting. That night, nearly everyone we
prayed for either said that their pain left, that it significantly
improved, or they were completely healed. Elijah, a human man
with a nature much like our own, prayed and God answered.
How much more effective should our prayers be under the New
Covenant, since the Holy Spirit now dwells within us?

Just prior to going on a mission trip to Romania in 1993,
God spoke a truth to me that I often remind myself and others.
The Lord said to me during prayer that day, "Bob, one man or
woman full of faith and the Holy Spirit can shake a nation." I
never shook the nation of Romania, but God was teaching me
something about faith and life in the Spirit before that trip.

Your mission is to bring resurrection life to situations that
are dead and need reviving. Both the Bible and church history
record the stories of ordinary men and women who have allowed
God to use them powerfully. Courageous faith and fullness of
the Spirit are required to do great exploits in his name (Dan.
11:32b). Elijah, as a human, could not birth or produce rain, yet
James 5:17-18 tells us that his prayers did. Your prayers have the
weight of heaven behind them; droughts cease, and situations
change when prayed according to God's will and pattern.

When your life is completely surrendered to Jesus and your motivation is to do only what you see the Father doing, then God can use you in remarkable ways—like impact a nation with his love and power. You can look on things that are dead and pray forth life. Effective prayer releases on earth, *as it is in heaven,* God's power—possibly to change the course of history—for you or someone else. You are a prayer, or breath, away from the release of his power to bring resurrection life to situations you face. Pray!

CHAPTER 10

Patient Endurance

—ᴟᴟ—

*"We can rejoice, too, when we run into problems and trials,
for we know that they help us develop endurance."*

— ROMANS 5:3 NLT

"Slow but steady wins the race." Aesop
"All great achievements require time."

— MAYA ANGELOU

SEE THE FINISH LINE

IN MY TWENTIES, I WAS an avid long-distance runner and I enjoyed training for 5K and 10K races. It was a terrific way to stay in shape and build friendships while I was in the military. Running long distance takes patient endurance—the training is lonely and requires keen mental focus. I was capable of winning or placing in my age category, which was respectable, but not fast enough to win first place for the overall race. However, there was one 5K race, on a hot Fourth of July day, that I did take first place overall.

A friend convinced me that we needed to run this race, as the field of runners looked thin. There was good reason for a small group of runners that day: north Florida is hot and humid in July, which is brutal for a road race. Long distance runners must have a penchant for pain! We left that day hopeful for a breeze and that we would place well. I also said a prayer, not to win, but to survive.

The day was extra hot and humid, and a field of about two hundred runners lined up for the race with us. I knew many of the top runners who showed up that day, and concluded that I had a chance to place well. I had been hydrating through the morning and felt confident I could survive this endurance run. I kept telling myself, "Don't start too fast. Be patient, pace yourself, and wait for the right moment to move on the leaders."

The gun sounded, and we started quickly. To my surprise, I found myself in a pack of about five men leading the field of runners. I had run enough races to know we were not on pace for a fantastic time, but I was content to be in the lead group as we neared the end of the first mile of our 3.1-mile race. As we approached the second mile marker, we were all sweating profusely, and my legs were feeling heavy as the lactic acid began to build up. Two of the men in our lead pack showed signs they were tiring and started to drop back. I thought to myself, "Man it's hot and my legs are hurting, but keep on pace and you can finish well."

As we crossed over the two-mile marker, a third man in our group dropped back. It was down to two of us contending for the lead, with only 1.1 mile to go. I knew we both were hot and tired, so it was going to come down to who was in better physical shape and who could mentally "see the finish line." The other runner moved up and took the lead, and it took everything in me to keep up with him. He was tall, lean, and in very good shape—a local doctor who was an excellent runner.

We rounded a corner and I could see the finish line straight ahead, about a half mile in the distance. I thought to myself, "I'm a good sprinter; I think I can out-sprint him for the last half mile." In my mind's eye, I could see myself placing first across the finish line and became confident that I could win. Despite my fatigue, I went for it—I started to run as fast as I could. He stayed right with me until the last one hundred yards, when I slowly pulled ahead of him and crossed the finish line in first place.

I had won my first 5K road race! All the pain and exhaustion was worth it. We congratulated each other on running a good race, drank some water, and picked up our trophies. I was surprised and elated, but more importantly, the lesson of patient endurance was reinforced within me. That day I also learned the value of visualizing a desired goal: "If you can see it, you can attain it."

Your Christian life is not a sprint, but an endurance run. There are seasons of quick growth and acceleration, but your walk with Jesus is a life-long journey. Endurance and persistence are required to finish strong—you must learn how to be strengthened in the Lord to finish your race well. As you learn to wait patiently on God's timing, your dreams can become reality.

REST IN GOD

In our demanding, type-A world, strength is not normally associated with rest. However, for the believer who understands that resting is a byproduct of living in Christ's victory, rest becomes powerful. Jesus has entered God's rest through his victory: "The one who entered God's rest also rested from his works, just as

God rested from his own" (Heb. 4:10 CEB). To fulfill your dreams and live your destiny, learning how to live from his victory, his rest, and his peace, is important.

In Christ, God has a complete and continual victory for you: "But thanks be to God, who always leads us in triumph in Christ..." (2 Cor. 2:14 NASB). The grace of Christ not only saves you, it also empowers you to live in his victory through the finished work of his death, resurrection, and ascension. Through his work, sin no longer controls you; rather, your union with Jesus in his ascension victory enables you to live as an overcomer. As you are presently positioned in Jesus, his victory brings you rest—his rest becomes your rest.

Learning to rest in God is not an abstract concept. Spiritual rest involves trusting God through *all* of life's circumstances. It strengthens you so that you can endure patiently, and empowers you to be full of God's peace and joy in the process. God's rest is eternal, and it is freely given through Christ—he is the Prince of Peace. You can rest because you are assured that with God, "all things work together for our good" (Rom. 8:28). For the believer who understands that we are living from his victory, peace and rest become normal attributes.

Does this mean that you will never work in God's kingdom? No, just the opposite—your life glorifies God through your good works (John 14:12; Eph. 2:10). These works flow from your life in Christ through the power of the Holy Spirit. Yet you no longer must strive for a breakthrough that Christ has already won. Instead, you learn to remain in the peace of God's presence and allow the Spirit to guide and empower you to do his work.

The greater you understand your authority in Christ and his finished work, the more confident you will be to remain at rest and overcome trials assertively. Trials and suffering are part of the Christian journey, but obstacles help build patient endurance (Rom. 5:1-5). Jesus demonstrated this as he confidently slept in the back of a boat during a severe storm. From his relationship with the Father, he could release God's peace and calm the storm. Because Jesus was one with the Father, the rest and peace of God was greater than the chaos around him. Storms come in this life, but God strengthens us to be at rest through life's journey. Building your foundation upon Christ, the solid rock, empowers you to weather any storm you may face.

For Paul, our position in Christ was not an abstract theological idea—it became an internal reality for him. Paul continually endured hardship and persecution for the gospel (2 Cor. 11:23-33). Despite the difficulties, his writings reflect growth in his understanding of God's complete love and care for him, regardless of his circumstances (Phil. 4:11-13). Paul was confident that God, through Jesus, would enable him to finish his mission and purpose. He reminded us that, "we must suffer many hardships to enter the kingdom of God" (Acts 14:22 NLT). To complete your destiny and purpose, you must endure the hardships that occur in life with patience. Your eyes must be set upon Jesus, the author and finisher of your faith. Christ embraced the suffering of the cross for the joy that awaited him (Heb. 12:2). Choose to remain in his joy and embrace suffering if necessary.

In Romans 8, Paul described the condition of the believer as a conqueror:

"[35]Who shall separate us from the love of Christ? Shall tribulation, or distress, or persecution, or famine, or nakedness, or peril, or sword? ...[37] Yet in all these things we are more than conquerors through Him who loved us. [38] For I am persuaded that neither death nor life, nor angels nor principalities nor powers, nor things present nor things to come, [39] nor height nor depth, nor any other created thing, shall be able to separate us from the love of God which is in Christ Jesus our Lord" (Rom. 8:35, 37-39).

The English phrase "more than conquerors" is derived from the Greek word *hupernikaō* which means, "one who is super victorious."[1] Through the victory of Jesus and your union with him, you are presently an overcomer and victorious—actually, super victorious! Understanding this truth at a heart level enables you to rest in his power and find peace in your journey.

A sign of your spiritual progress is your realization that you are the very temple of God, and are living from your new life in Christ through his victory and rest. Paul wrote to the Colossians, "Christ in you, the hope of glory" (Col. 1:27). The strength and glory of Christ is within you by the indwelling of the Holy Spirit; learn to allow the greater one to keep you in his peace, patience, and strength. Further, understand that his power is greatly at work within you to accomplish more than is humanly possible. Twentieth-century Christian mystic Sadhu Sundar Singh wrote, "Then did I know that man's heart is the very throne and Citadel of God, and that when He (Christ) enters there to abide, heaven begins."[2] This is heaven on earth: his peace, joy, and rest begin to manifest in your heart when you recognize and embrace the reality of Jesus' victory and his indwelling empowerment by the Holy Spirit.

You're Being Laid Off Today!

Several years ago, Carolyn was laid off from her job as a contract software engineer for a large aerospace company in Melbourne,

FL, where we were living at the time. We funded much of our short-term mission work during this season with money we both earned; we were modern-day "tentmakers" to further the gospel (Acts 18:2-4). Her job loss came as a sudden shock to us, but God was faithful even through the layoff process and subsequent financial changes.

As she walked into work that day, the Lord spoke to her, "Today, you will be laid off from your job. But don't worry." She went to her desk knowing that God revealed what was about to happen, and she remained at peace. After lunch, she went into the computer lab to help correct problems with the software she and her colleagues were working on. One of the team members remarked, "Boy, I don't know what we would do without your help on this project!" She thought to herself, "Well, you better be prepared to finish without me!"

While she was in the lab, she received a phone call from her supervisor requesting that she return to her desk. When she arrived, the supervisor and someone from security were waiting to inform her that her job had been terminated. She was instructed to log off her computer, sign her time card, pack her personal belongings into an empty box, and then was politely escorted from the building. Carolyn remained at peace through the entire process because she knew that God was allowing this. However, her layoff still felt like a rejection. She had done nothing wrong; the company was simply reducing the size of their work force as the project neared completion.

Carolyn's salary was about half of our income at the time and we had to quickly adjust our budget in order to compensate for the loss. Yet God also abundantly provided. For the next several months, she received a generous unemployment check which helped us during the transition. Ironically, before the layoff, we considered having Carolyn leave her job to stay home with our daughter, Hannah. So, what came as a shock was the hand of God giving us the desire of our hearts for our daughter. Carolyn could now take care of Hannah instead of using a daycare—a tremendous blessing for all of us.

God truly had something better for Carolyn, and what looked like a setback was his grace. Sometimes God closes a door to move you through another one. Through that experience we learned the value of waiting upon God in complete trust.

God never promises that life will be free of trials—he promises that he will be with you always. In the book of Nahum, the prophet declares, "The LORD is good, a stronghold in the day of trouble; and He knows those who trust in Him" (Nah. 1:7). If you doubt God's goodness during adversity, you will spiral downward into negativity. You may lose hope for a bright future; worse, you may walk away from Jesus. Learning how to wait upon God—even when situations are overwhelming, and answers are delayed—is a key to walking victoriously in Christian life. To believe that God is good through all of life's situations is essential to walking in peace and security in this life, with complete trust and patience while you wait. Trusting God through uncertainty is a hallmark of Christian maturity.

Trusting in God's Goodness from a Renewed Perspective

Trust is defined as "belief that someone or something is reliable, good, honest, effective, etc."[3] It is having an assured confidence and trust in the character and the ability of the one making the promise. Your ability to trust God confidently relates to your revelation of his character and promises. When trials and circumstances occur in life, you may be tempted to rely on human understanding apart from complete faith in God. Proverbs states, "When people do not accept divine guidance, they run wild" (Prov. 29:18 NLT). Without a deepening understanding of the character and goodness of God, your mind may wander, even run to wrong conclusions about God and his nature. A renewed perspective of the character of God and his promises is essential to trusting his divine guidance when things in life "go south."

Proverbs also underscores the importance of keeping your mind anchored in God's truth and revelation: "⁵ Trust in the LORD with all your heart; do not depend on your own understanding. ⁶ Seek his will in all you do, and he will show you which path to take" (Prov. 3:5-6 NLT). We are instructed *not* to depend on our understanding. Your understanding needs to come by the Spirit of God, not from human reasoning or your current situation. A mind that is unrenewed to God's truth will look at the natural circumstances and conclude the situation is impossible. The Bible is full of examples of those who doubted God and were unable to realize his promises to them. Your circumstances do not determine God's nature and ability; rather, your trust in God releases his grace to answer and affect change. Trust in God completely—it silences doubt.

DESIRE HIS PRESENCE

A vital key to developing a stronger trust and deeper understanding of God and his goodness is to spend time daily with him in worship, prayer, and the Word. David was a great king, warrior, and prophetic voice. God said of him, "he is a man after my own heart." David had become a lover of God's presence, someone who spent time with him frequently in worship and prayer.

As I described earlier, real prayer is communion and two-way dialogue with God, where we learn to hear from him as much as we petition him. Through this lifestyle, David became confident in God, and knew that God would deliver him in all of life's situations—even when he sinned. He desired to be in the presence of God, not because of formalized religion, but because of ongoing encounters with God. God's presence became the sincere passion of his life. David said regarding his desire for God's presence:

> "One thing I have desired of the LORD, that will I seek: That I may dwell in the house of the LORD all the days of my life, to behold the beauty of the LORD, and to inquire in His temple. For in the time of trouble He shall hide me in His pavilion; in the secret place of His tabernacle He shall hide me; He shall set me high upon a rock" (Psalm 27:4-5).

David was convinced he would see the goodness of the Lord in his life and therefore was able to wait patiently upon God despite contrary circumstances. David declared, "I would have lost heart, unless I had believed that I would see the goodness of the LORD in the land of the living" (Psalm 27:13). Abiding in the presence of the Lord as a lifestyle builds your confidence and trust in God. His presence and word begin to shape your internal reality to believe God is good—he has your best interest in mind.

BELIEVE IN GOD'S GOODNESS—ALWAYS!

I went through difficult seasons as a young Christian, and Psalm 27:13 became a "life verse" for me. It has continued to strengthen and sustain me in my walk with God—through the highs and lows of my life. I discovered in God's Word and through personal experience that our heavenly Father is a loving, benevolent God who desires to bless us with his goodness, comfort, peace, and joy. Being fully convinced of this will strengthen the willingness of your heart to wait patiently upon God.

Hebrews 11 recounts many heroes of the faith. This chapter describes the faith of godly heroes, ordinary people who have gone on before us and trusted God in difficult circumstances. Toward the end of the chapter, the Holy Spirit reveals something to us through their lives: not all of them saw their desires fulfilled on this side of eternity. They died in faith holding on to the promises God gave them: "All these people earned a good reputation because of their faith, yet none of them received all that God had promised" (Heb. 11:39 NLT).

One of the tensions in God's kingdom is simply that not all prayers are answered, not all dreams are fulfilled, some people suffer as they follow God, and some leave earth with promises "unrealized." I know firsthand the disappointment of prayer that seems unanswered, having lost both of my parents to cancer at an early age—despite our prayer for their healing. Yet, the greater eternal reality is that through the cross of Christ and our resurrection hope in him, I will see them again. You must know confidently that despite seasons of seeming contradiction to God's nature and promises, God is always good. When you can declare like Job, "Though He slay me, yet will I trust Him" (Job 13:15), you have reached a place of enduring faith in God that will sustain you through all of life's situations.

There are times when we can be confident that we know the will of God, pray in faith, and stand firmly on God's promise, but the prayer is not answered as we anticipate. Perhaps you are praying for a financial breakthrough or healing miracle, only to lose a job, end up bankrupt, or like me, lose a loved one to disease. Whatever your demanding situation, it is imperative that you believe God is good and can trust him unreservedly. Keep your focus on Jesus and trust in your future resurrection—this is the foundational hope of every Christian.

Some situations and circumstances simply cannot be explained in life. Promises and dreams seem unfulfilled at times, as we read in Hebrews 11. Don't let your love grow cold or allow your heart to become bitter toward God. Trust him always—it is wrong to assume we understand all the ways and mysteries of God. Many have walked away from relationship with Jesus because of the "mystery of faith" when circumstances seem to contradict his Word and nature. Remember his thoughts and ways are higher than ours (Isa. 55:8-9).

PATIENCE AS YOU WAIT

Let's continue with David. He went on to say in Psalm 27:14, "Wait on the LORD; be of good courage, and He shall strengthen your heart; Wait, I say, on the LORD!" David, from his revelation of God's goodness, knew that despite seemingly hopeless situations, he could wait confidently on the Lord in every circumstance. David reaffirms his calm resolve to trust God patiently in Psalm 62:

"⁵ My soul, wait silently for God alone, For my expectation *is* from Him. ⁶ He only *is* my rock and my salvation; *He is* my defense; I shall not be moved. ⁷ In God *is* my salvation and my glory; The rock of my strength, *And* my refuge, *is* in God" (Psalm 62:5-7).

Psalm 27:14 and 62:5 both describe waiting. The English word "wait" is translated from the Hebrew word *qâvâh*. It means to wait, to look patiently for, and to bind together by twisting.⁴ Let us first look at the aspect of patience with *qâvâh*, and then we will examine what it means to "bind or twist together."

Just as David learned, the writer of Hebrews explained that as we develop the practice of waiting upon God through patient endurance, we receive his promises: "do not become sluggish, but imitate those who through faith and patience inherit the promises" (Heb. 6:12). The Amplified Version of this verse reads, "...and by practice of patient endurance and waiting are [now] inheriting the promises." (AMPCE) The practice of patient endurance is a skill that is developed through a daily and consistent walk with God.

Patience undergirds your faith; it is an essential quality of the Spirit needed to maintain your poise through the trials of life and as you wait for the manifestation of the promises of God in the natural realm. Faith is substance—it is evidence of that which is to come. Patience sustains you while you wait confidently for the manifestation of your faith.

TWISTED TOGETHER

Perhaps the most interesting interpretation of this word *qâvâh* is that of "binding together by twisting." This aspect of the word *qâvâh* can be illustrated by trees whose trunks grow up from the same roots, but they are twisted together or intertwined (a good example of this is a rubber tree). When you wait upon the Lord, you are binding yourself to him. You are twisting yourself around his character, nature, and promises—much like the tree whose trunks are twisted and bound together in an inseparable fashion.

In Isaiah 40:31 we see *qâvâh* used once again. The Amplified Bible reads:

"[29] He gives power (*kōaḥ*) to the faint and weary and to him who has no might He increases strength [causing it to multiply and making it to abound]. [30] Even youths shall faint and be weary, and [selected] young men shall feebly stumble and fall exhausted; [31] But those who wait (*qâvâh*) for the Lord [who expect, look for, and hope in Him] shall change and renew their strength and power; they shall lift their wings and mount up [close to God] as eagles [mount up to the sun]; they shall run and not be weary, they shall walk and not faint or become tired" (Isa. 40:29-31 AMPCE).

The word "power" in Isaiah 40:29 comes from the Hebrew word *kōaḥ*, which means "divine power, ability, substance, wealth, or divine strength to lay hold of something that is beyond our strength to lay hold of."[5] We could read verse 29 this way: "He gives power (*kōaḥ*), divine ability, substance, wealth or strength for those who are weak, exhausted, weary or even infirmed, which is the inability to produce results."

In Deuteronomy 8:18, Moses states, "for it is He who gives you power (*kōaḥ*) to get wealth... that He may establish (confirm) His covenant with you." God gives *kōaḥ* to get wealth for those who wait upon him. However, it is much more than wealth.

God gives *kōaḥ*, or divine ability, to receive healing, deliverance, and restoration.

Something happens inside of you when you bind yourself to the Lord through the process of waiting upon him. There is a renewing and an altering taking place inside of you. You become more like Jesus by the power of the Holy Spirit. You begin to function out of his nature, out of his power, and out of his faith. There is a divine exchange that takes place, which causes you to break forth into the power of heaven, far beyond earthly limitations.

Often, some of your most intuitive and creative moments will come to you by the Spirit as you *qâvâh*, bind yourself to the Lord and wait patiently. As you *qâvâh* (bind or twist) yourself with the Lord, then his *kōaḥ* (divine power) becomes active and changes you because God's kingdom is in you. Jesus and his kingdom begin to work in and through your life. Your inner world transforms, and suddenly, "you shall renew your strength."

Your capacity to reproduce, your abilities, your strength, your substance, your wealth—all of this shifts under the influence of heaven. When you remain in God, patiently waiting upon him, divine encounters happen, the *kōaḥ* of God comes and there is a transformation in your life. This is how God can take ordinary people and suddenly give them the capacity to do "exploits in his name."

As you wait upon God, his divine power is at work to change impossible situations and bring heaven's reality to earth. "Wait on the LORD; be of good courage, and He shall strengthen your heart; Wait, I say, on the LORD!" (Psalm 27:14)—for he is good!

CHAPTER 11

Overcoming the Obstacles

—ᴠᴠ—

"Nothing is impossible for God."

— *Luke 1:37 CEB*

*"Obstacles are those frightful things you see
when you take your eyes off your goals."*

— *Henry Ford*

The River is Raging

Faith flows from an intimate and loving relationship with God. A life of faith is not about achieving results, but living as one who obeys, not out of duty, but as a lover who trusts the One who guides. When God directs, faith ignores the natural circumstances and sees the opportunity to live in promised inheritance. Your ability to trust Jesus confidently amid the uncertainties of life will determine how much you abide in God's peace, joy, and victory. Courageous faith sees opportunity in contradiction. It is a faith which can deflect chaos and release God's peace in a turbulent world.

The river is raging. You have a word from the Lord: "Cross over." What do you do? The river is about to flood and is perhaps a mile wide. Do you obey God? Or do you rely on your natural understanding of the situation and use common sense?

The story I am referring to happened to Joshua and the children of Israel. Forty years prior, God invited Israel to possess their inheritance in the Promised Land. Unbelief robbed a generation, with the exception of Joshua and Caleb. Forty years later, Moses had died and God directed Joshua to "cross over." The Jordon River was at flood stage. In the natural, it did not seem to be the right time—the river was a mile wide. However, with Jesus, obstacles become opportunities when he is leading.

GRACE EMPOWERS

The Lord told Joshua three times to "be strong and of good courage." The phrase "be strong" is from the Hebrew *châzaq*, which means: courageous, valiant, manly, strengthened, established, firm, fortified, obstinate, and mighty.[1] Yet not only was God giving Joshua instructions how to be strong (Jos. 1:8-9), but the command to "be strong and courageous" also imparted the strength and courage to obey and realize the promise. God gave a "grace" to Joshua in his command. Prophetic declaration releases God's power to do the impossible.

Another example of the word *châzaq* and the concept to "be strong" is found in the book of Samuel, when David and his men were defeated at Ziklag: "Now David was greatly distressed, for the people spoke of stoning him, because the soul of all the people was grieved, every man for his sons and his daughters. But David strengthened himself in the Lord his God" (1 Sam. 30:6). David strengthened himself, or literally "made himself strong" in

God. He knew that to overcome obstacles he had to strengthen himself in the Lord. David drew on God's empowering grace through prayer, worship, and God's Word to be strong.

Grace is much more than forgiveness; it empowers you to be who you are not. You are becoming like Christ because of the power of the Holy Spirit, who is the agent of grace. Grace infuses life and power within you to become your identity and to do what God has asked you to do.

Paul wrote in Ephesians to "be strong in the Lord and in the power of His might" (Eph. 6:10). The phrase "be strong in the Lord" could instead read "strengthen yourself in the Lord." Your strength is found in the Lord, in his greatness, authority, and victory through Christ. True, it is faith in his grace that restores your relationship with God (Eph. 2:8-9). However, it is also God's empowering grace by the Spirit that enables you to achieve good works in Christ (Eph. 2:10), and fulfill dreams and destiny. His grace empowers you to overcome the challenges in your journey.

Joshua, David, and Paul learned how to strengthen themselves in the Lord, and this concept is vital for us today too. They were intentional in their relationship with God and to walk in his victory as overcomers. To complete your assignment and fulfill your destiny, you must learn how to stay strong in the Lord as you move forward in life.

YOUR JOB IS YOUR JORDAN

A year after we planted Passion Church, the Lord challenged me to "cross over." I was a bi-vocational pastor, working a full-time job as an electrical engineer to support my family while pastoring the new church. During that time, the church grew but it was not enough to support a full-time pastor. In fact, we were the main financial givers in the church, but we gave and labored with joy—we were following Jesus.

During this season, the Lord prompted me to take a mission trip to Brazil with Global Awakening. It was another step of faith, as our personal and church finances were tight, but I went. The trip was powerful. The Spirit of God was moving in extraordinary ways both within the team and in the churches where we ministered. We saw many people come to Christ and many more receive healing.

During the trip, one morning we had a time of training and prayer for pastors and leaders. Afterwards, along with many of the Brazilian leaders, I found myself prostrate on the floor crying out to God and consecrating my life and ministry afresh to the Lord. God's tangible presence was heavy upon me. I can still see the floor of the church in Rio de Janeiro as I write—it became holy ground for me.

As I lay yielded to God at that moment, the Holy Spirit spoke to me, "Bob, your job is your river Jordan and I need you to 'cross over.' The church cannot become what I intend it to be until you leave your job and pastor full-time." I was undone, shaken, and nervous. I knew God's voice and I was sure this was him speaking, but what he had just spoken challenged me.

I was making an excellent salary with good benefits as an engineer. We had money in savings, but not enough to sustain us for very long. Yet I kept hearing, "Bob, your job is your river Jordan and I need you to 'cross over.'" Oswald Chambers once said, "Faith doesn't know where it is being led, but it loves and knows the one who is leading." True faith responds out of relationship and obeys God's guidance—no matter how bizarre. Faith does not rely on the natural senses or the wisdom of man to decide when to respond to God. It hears and obeys.

When I arrived home from the mission trip, I immediately shared this experience with Carolyn. To my surprise, she calmly said to me, "Before you left, God had been preparing me that you might be leaving your job soon." I think she had more faith at that moment than I did. We both continued to pray and seek God for confirmation during the next few weeks. Each time we prayed, we sensed that this was God's will and that I was to leave my comfortable and secure job.

I spoke to my supervisor at work, explaining to him about the church we started two years prior, and that I needed to attend to it full-time. To my surprise, he was supportive in my decision. He offered me a part-time position, but as we prayed, God reaffirmed to us that he needed us at the church full-time. With some trepidation, I turned in my notice to leave the company. We trusted that "as God guides, he provides," and provide he did.

Our savings ran out within a few months, but the church had grown and was able to pay me a small salary. God was providing. Random people would show up at our home at odd times with groceries. God continued to provide. By faith, we hired a worship leader and moved him and his family across the country to Tucson. Somehow, all the bills were paid and God kept providing. As I shared earlier, God directed us to purchase church property during this season. God was in the details, and all he needed was for us to trust and obey him. He kept providing.

I am convinced that our church and our ministry is where it is today because we said "yes" to God when he asked me to leave the job. Our promised land was on the other side; we just had to trust God and cross over. Crossing rivers can be daunting, but when Jesus is the one making the way, you will get across to your promised land. Your yes to God is all that he needs—let your yes be louder than doubt and unbelief!

What has God asked you to do? What river or impossible situation are you facing today? It may seem impossible in the natural, but his promise and grace will empower you to obtain what he is offering. When the children of Israel stepped into the raging waters of the Jordon River, it was then that the water stopped and they were able to cross over. Grace empowers you to believe, obey, and possess promises despite circumstances. The Lord is empowering many in this hour to cross over and realize their promised inheritance. He is giving you the grace to cross over in this season—trust him.

POSSESSING PROMISED INHERITANCE

An entire generation of Israel wandered for forty years in the desert because they were unable to trust God and his promise of inheritance. That generation longed for the Promised Land, but they died dreaming about it, except for Joshua and Caleb. The skepticism of an unbelieving generation turned the Promised Land into a dream that never materialized.

During those same forty years, Joshua and Caleb developed within themselves a victorious mindset. When God commissioned Joshua, he responded faithfully and turned the dreams and hopes of others into land, cities, homes, and possessions—an inheritance for generations to come. At 85 years old, Caleb took possession of his promised territory, proving that tenacious faith endures desert years to realize nurtured promises and dreams.

Why did Joshua succeed? What were the key factors that enabled him to overcome the obstacles in his way? Joshua's heart attitude provides the answer. God formed Joshua's perspective, and challenges did not hinder his perception of the promises. He wasn't swayed by bad news or circumstances.

An understanding of God and his promises is the difference between what happens for some people and what does not happen for others. Your success is in God, his Word, and how you apply his promises. Circumstances do not dictate whether you have victory; your perception and faith do. Like Joshua and Caleb, you are nurturing a victory inside of you—if you have the confidence to trust God through the journey. Those who accomplish remarkable things and live extraordinary lives allow God to form their internal reality and perception of life.

Here are five factors behind Joshua's success, which provide principles to overcoming obstacles and fulfilling your dreams.

1. GOD IS YOUR STRENGTH

The New Testament makes this all-inclusive promise twice: "With God all things are possible" (Matt. 19:26, Mark 10:27). Note the preposition *with*. All things are possible for you, *with* God. Your strength and ability to overcome obstacles is a result of your relationship with God—apart from him, you are limited in your ability to address life's challenges.

Joshua entered Canaan triumphantly because he knew God and trusted his promises, not because he had a great army—they were descendants of slaves. God told Joshua, "Every place that the sole of your foot will tread upon, I have given you" (Josh. 1:3). Notice that the promise is past tense. God expected Joshua to act on what he had revealed, knowing that God had already gone before him and would be with him.

Like Joshua, God expects you to believe and act upon what he has revealed to you, in both his written Word and through what the Holy Spirit has spoken to you. Because God is with you always, he has the right to ask the impossible of you—he is your strength and source. Obstacles move, and those who trust in and rely solely upon God receive his inheritance.

2. BELIEVE GOD'S PROMISES

God had already given the land of Canaan to the children of Israel. "From the wilderness ... to the going down of the sun, shall be your territory" (Josh. 1:4). Joshua and the people had to determine how much land they would go in and occupy. It was theirs by faith, and it happened when they decided to act in obedience.

Joshua's faith and courage opened the door to receive the fulfillment of promises and make history. The Israelites had to cross the river Jordan and take the gift that God offered. As God promised, they had to tread with the "sole of their feet" upon the land they desired to receive from God. They had to look past the walled cities and giants that were in the land—these were mere speed bumps on the road to fulfilled destiny.

God's Word is for you, and you can receive it as though he spoke it to you personally. Your only requirement is to believe and act on his promises by faith. The promises of scripture create action in a believing heart. There is a divine principal, "Seek and you shall find; knock and it shall be opened." What has God promised you? How much of the kingdom is available? How much have you made up in your mind to have in God? There are realms available in God's kingdom that can be achieved only as you determine to possess and occupy the territory with God.

3. PURSUE GOD'S VISION

What is the vision God has given you for your life, your family, your church, or where you work? Sometimes your individual breakthrough connects to a corporate mission. Vision is not automatic—if you are not looking and leaning into the vision God is revealing, you will not see it. "The secret things belong to the LORD our God. The revealed things belong to us and to our children forever..." (Deut. 29:29 CEB). You are responsible for what God has unveiled—act confidently upon his revealed will.

Purity of heart empowers vision. Jesus said, "Blessed are the pure in heart, for they shall see God" (Matt. 5:8). In Christ, you are made pure and holy, and he is your sanctification and righteousness (1 Cor. 1:30). However, you are also to pursue a holy life and allow yourself to be transformed into his image (2 Cor. 7:1). You are to be clothed in your "new man," which is the very righteousness of Christ that is perfecting and establishing you.

To realize God's vision, pursue purity. Give no place for the enemy to accuse you or ensnare you. You will be more confident and there will be no hindrance to your prayers: "If I had not confessed the sin in my heart, the Lord would not have listened. (Psalm 66:18 NLT).

While you pursue purity of heart, realize that God is with you always. Many have an ungodly belief that God's presence and revelation is greater for some people than for others. However, from the beginning God said, "I will not leave you nor forsake you" (Josh. 1:5). He promised this to Joshua and repeated the same statement 1,300 years later by the writer of Hebrews: "I will never leave you nor forsake you" (Heb. 13:5). God has committed himself to you, not because you are good or because your faith is perfect. Rather, it is because you are his child and he is your loving Father.

God is with you through the highs and lows of life—not just when you have success—otherwise, achievement would never come. You are valuable to God. The Father placed the Holy

Spirit within you to empower you to fulfill dreams and purpose for your life.

4. POSITIONED IN GOD

Remember, God is with you always and will never leave you. Your circumstances do not have to be your reality, because God is your circumstance. Do not wait for all the right conditions, for they will never come. You can expect Jesus to release favor and create opportunities as you walk faithfully with him. God brought the walls of Jericho down for Joshua and the children of Israel because he was with them and they obeyed God's directive.

The "Hall of Faith" (Hebrews 11) and church history demonstrate that others before you took advantage of the truth that God is your circumstance. They believed this principle and acted on it. They refused to give into fear but acted in faith upon God's revealed will. Like Joshua, you can go in the name of Lord with the same courage God imparted to him (Josh.1:6-7, 9).

As I mentioned in an earlier chapter, understand your identity and position in Christ. You are united with Christ in his death, burial, resurrection, and ascension (Rom. 6:4-5; Eph. 2:6). Further, you are now a child of God and a citizen of heaven. Your identity and lineage are in God's family now (Rom. 8:14-17; Gal. 3:26-27).

Your strength is found in Jesus and in his power: "be strong in the Lord and in the power of His might" (Eph. 6:10). The key is in the phrase "in the Lord." It means God's supernatural power is found in one place—in the Lord. The power is located or contained in Jesus Christ. The reason God's power is accessible to you is that both his divine power and you are in the same place. The power is located inside the Lord, and you are also located inside the Lord. You are united with Christ and with God's power.

The same Greek locative case that describes God's power located inside Jesus is used nine times in Ephesians 1. Paul says that we are "in him," "in Christ," "in whom" or "in the beloved" (Eph. 1:3, 4,6,7,10,11, and 13). Each of these occurrences is also in the locative case. Paul is saying we are placed in Jesus, and that he has become our realm of existence and the place of our habitation. Just as you live at a certain physical address, you also have a spiritual address. As a believer you permanently reside in the Son of God, secure in him.

Here is a great illustration of this truth using an aquarium. For simplicity, picture an aquarium with just a tank, water, and fish. The water and fish are different in substance, but they both reside in the same tank. The tank serves as the home for both of these two substances. The fish (the believer) does not have to release its faith to get into the water (God's power), for it already lives in the water, housed by the tank (Christ). The aquarium is a simple metaphor that illustrates how you and I are located inside the Lord with his power—the Holy Spirit!

Jesus tells us in Matthew's gospel that the "gates of hell will not prevail against the church" (Matt. 16:18). In ancient cities, gates kept out advancing armies, unless they broke through the gate. Jesus has defeated the powers of darkness and removed the enemy's gate. The powers of hell may roar, but you need to remember that you serve the living God, and nothing is impossible with him—his kingdom is expanding and advancing. The enemy is fearful of God's people who understand Jesus is their authority and circumstance.

5. ACT ON GOD'S WORD

With little forewarning, God gave Joshua a "suddenly" when he told him that they would cross the Jordan River to possess the land within three days (Josh. 1:11). Israel had been on the east side of the Jordan for an entire generation. They were grasshoppers in their own sight, believing that it was impossible for them to occupy the Promised Land (Num. 13:33). Their children had to unlearn the slave mentality of their parents and follow Joshua confidently to receive the inheritance promised by God. Unbelief can rob you of your promised inheritance.

If you think you are a grasshopper, then you are, because as a person "thinks in his heart, so is he" (Prov. 23:7). However, in God you are no longer a grasshopper—no longer a slave—ever. You are never alone, never abandoned, and always on the winning side with God. The challenges you face are opportunities for God. Winston Churchill once said, "A pessimist sees the difficulty in every opportunity; an optimist sees the opportunity in every difficulty."

When God called Joshua, what was happening within Israel is that the nation was grieving. "The Lord [said] to Joshua: 'Moses ... is dead. Now, therefore, arise, go'" (Josh. 1:1-2). What a moment for destiny to unfold—with the funeral of their leader. It was a disastrous hour for Joshua and the people of Israel. It may have seemed like the vision died with Moses. However, God specializes in bringing life out of death. Sometimes it is in the transition and the uncertainty of the hour that God's purposes begin to unfold and become the clearest.

I have discovered that when I begin my day with worship and prayer, fresh vision and purpose become the clearest. This is especially true during seasons of transition. I meditate on his Word while praying and worshipping. I discover that I am strengthened in the Lord. I become confident and ready to act upon what God has promised and revealed. During these moments, the Spirit fans into flame my love for God (2 Tim. 1:6).

Sometimes I must offer a sacrifice of praise. My human nature may not feel like worshipping God, but my spirit longs to draw near to him once again. I choose then to push past my fleshly nature and draw near to God. Sometimes, those are the days that his presence is the most tangible and I find myself strengthened significantly.

Be obedient to God's revealed will. James says that faith is demonstrated by works (Jam. 2:22-26), and God honors faith that is born out of obedience. This may take many forms. Be proactive—find a place to serve in the body of Christ. Be missionally minded—reach others with God's love and power. Get training and education—position yourself for breakthrough and promotion. Never stop learning; never stop growing in knowledge, ability, or in the things of the Spirit.

Obedience is also affected by how well you take care of your body. Take care of yourself and get proper rest, nutrition, and exercise. Prolonged fatigue and or illness will affect your emotional state and ability to fulfill your kingdom assignment. Even after his great victory on Mt. Carmel, Elijah became weary, discouraged, and disillusioned. He was ready to quit the race and give up on his calling (1 Kings 19:3-10). God knew he was weary, and that he needed to recharge spiritually as much as he needed emotional and physical rest. Do not allow yourself to reach a place of burnout; it can be challenging to recover. However, if you find yourself in that place, be proactive and get rest, adjust your diet, exercise, and spiritually recharge. Remember, "David strengthened himself in the Lord."

The Holy Spirit is near to us—open your heart and receive by faith his refreshing and strengthening today. God has designed our lives in Christ such that it would be strange for us not to receive his power and strength in order to live victoriously. There is no need to beg, plead, or beat yourself up in prayer in order to convince yourself that you are good enough to receive his strength. If you know Jesus, you are already in the same place with him and with his power.

Moses, My Servant, is Dead

Prior to moving to Arizona in 2001, we were in transition. We moved from Florida to Pennsylvania in 2000, with the intent to partner with a church that would send us as missionaries to oversee a church and orphanage in rural Romania. Unable to sell our house in Florida, we rented it and moved into a rental house in Pennsylvania. After we settled, I returned to Florida to work the last two weeks of my job—I know what modern day "tent making" to fund ministry is about. We were excited about the upcoming mission work in Romania, but God had other plans.

When I arrived back in Pennsylvania, I took a temporary job as a bookkeeper making a whopping ten dollars an hour—and we were grateful. Carolyn began cleaning houses to help with our family expenses as we prepared to go to Romania. Some of the homes belonged to her high school classmates—nothing like cleaning the toilets of high school peers to keep you humble and close to God. Those nine months in PA proved to be a time of uncertainty, trial, and gestation—God was about to birth something.

Five months into my bookkeeping assignment, my employer gave me the good and bad news. The good news was that I corrected their bookkeeping, which was months behind. The bad news was,

"We no longer need you." There went my job. Carolyn kept cleaning houses and we waited on God for the new season to unfold. I spent the next few weeks praying at home. It was a long, cold winter.

I was struggling and feeling discouraged. Not only had I lost my meager job, but the future mission work suddenly changed: the church no longer needed us to go to Romania. While we were preparing to go, they had temporarily put a Romanian pastor in place, skeptical that he could do the work. They were wrong—he did an excellent job and the church and orphanage were flourishing under his leadership. I began looking for another job and seeking God for new direction. It seemed like we had taken a wrong turn—but God.

On one of those cold afternoons, I was sitting in my chair praying and watching the snow through my living room window while I held Rapha, the family cat. In my spirit, I heard the Lord say, "Moses my servant is dead, arise, and go." I knew this was the Holy Spirit speaking but questions flooded my mind. "What God? Who is Moses? Go where? Do what?" Of course, I knew the story of Moses and Joshua, but I could not piece together how this applied to me. God gave me no answers that day—but he positioned me for what was to come next.

Within the next few weeks, I received two job offers in different parts of the country. Neither was back in Florida, as God was closing doors there. One of the jobs was an engineering position in Tucson, AZ. After flying here for a job interview in the spring of 2001, the company made an excellent job offer, with a cash-signing bonus, good benefits, and a solid relocation package. They even increased the cash bonus after I asked them for more—I was testing the waters.

After much prayer and deliberation, Carolyn and I said yes to the offer in Tucson. After accepting the job, the next day the

Lord said to me while I was praying, "Bob, you will excel in the job there; your family will flourish, and your ministry will prosper in Tucson. I can make streams in the desert." God has done all those things—just as he promised. Overnight, we went from the cold to a warm desert—it was God's plan—and yes, it is a dry heat!

Within months, we started the church in Tucson, as I shared earlier. It was later, while pastoring, that I began to understand what God spoke to me that cold snowy afternoon years prior, "Moses my servant is dead, arise, and go." God was preparing me to move to Tucson and establish the church. He was imparting strength and courage to enable me to cross over the river of uncertainty. What seemed like a time of anxiety, even a funeral of sorts, was actually a launching pad for greater things—for us and those we would lead.

Remember, God is your success—he is your circumstance. Jesus is your champion and breakthrough. Cast off any feelings of inferiority and discouragement. Joshua succeeded because he understood that the same God who was with Moses was with him. The same God is with you and he will never leave you nor forsake you.

Obstacles are often opportunities in disguise. With God, all things are possible. When Jesus is leading, you can safely trust him through every transition and season of uncertainty. Extraordinary people recognize that problems are often platforms for promotion. Dreams are frequently realized when the circumstances seem the most daunting.

CHAPTER 12

The Tale of Two Dreams

—◦◦◦—

"Hope deferred makes the heart sick,
but a dream fulfilled is a tree of life."

— PROVERBS 13:12 NLT

"When it comes to their dreams, truly successful
people have enough creativity to think it out,
and enough character to try it out."

—JOHN MAXWELL

TWO DREAMERS

THE STORY OF DAVID AND Jonathan is fascinating. Like each of us, they were created uniquely and born into different families. Each had a destiny and a dream to fulfill. They were both imperfect. Both loved God, loved their nation, desired to serve, and dreamed of success in life. They were best friends and were committed to each other's success.

Jonathan was born into privilege; King Saul was Jonathan's father. He had wealth, reputation, and favor in the royal palace.

In Middle Eastern culture during that time, the family would continue the King's dynasty. Jonathan, a prince in the kingdom, had a bright future ahead of him. However, Saul disobeyed God and the Lord removed his hand of favor from him. God determined to have another king and, suddenly, Jonathan's future changed.

God sent the prophet Samuel to anoint the next king of Israel—a young teenage shepherd boy named David. Little did David know that after he was anointed by Samuel, he would spend the next several years in the wilderness hiding from Saul, and that this was the first of three anointings that would take place in his life. Seven years later David was anointed king over Judah (2 Sam 2:4), and then another seven years passed before he was anointed king over all of Israel (2 Sam 5:3-4).

Suddenly David, the youngest and apparently least respected of Jesse's sons, was promoted by God to be the next king. Some scholars believe that David was an illegitimate son of Jesse, for David declared in the Psalms, "Behold, I was brought forth in iniquity, and in sin my mother conceived me" (Psalm 51:5). Often, those who are marginalized and considered the least are best positioned to rule with God. Humility precedes honor; it is a tree of life.

Almost from the beginning of David's journey, Jonathan's heart united with David (1 Sam. 18:1-4). When Saul realized God's Spirit had departed from him and rested upon David, he became insanely jealous, even desiring to kill David. Jonathan risked his own life to defend David and help him escape. Jonathan was willing to lay his future aside for God's purposes. He recognized God's hand, favor, and anointing upon David.

A new dynasty was forming, and Jonathan—unlike most sons of nobility—helped his friend and future king of Israel. While hiding in the wilderness, Jonathan said to David, "Do not fear, for the hand of Saul my father shall not find you. You shall be king over Israel, and I shall be next to you. Even my father Saul knows that" (1 Sam. 23:17). Jonathan recognized that it was David who was destined to be the next king, not Jonathan or any of his brothers. His dream was to help David and to be the number-two man in the future Davidic kingdom of Israel.

During that moment, David and Jonathan reaffirmed their commitment to each other and reminded each other of their future and destiny. What was needed for David and Jonathan to succeed and fulfill their purpose?

BELIEVE IN YOUR DREAM

To see your dreams fulfilled, believe God is with you, believe in your dream, and believe in your ability to succeed. David saw himself as the next king of Israel. He believed God chose him for this purpose. His encounter with God through the anointing he received from Samuel empowered him to succeed against Goliath and the Philistines, and inspired him and convinced him of his calling. Though Saul tried for years to kill him and pursued him through the wilderness, David believed in the promise and the dream God gave him. Despite hardships and setbacks, David refused to allow circumstances to rob him of God's promises.

Jonathan also knew his calling, and with a servant's heart he was willing to take a subordinate role in the kingdom—his future. During those wilderness years he helped David whenever he could. He believed in what God had for him and for David in the coming kingdom. As much as David, Jonathan could envision the future and the dream unfold. Both men knew that God was with them. Assured of God's promises, they were willing to serve others and each other to see their dream become a reality. The vision sustained them through years of adversity as they walked faithfully with God and each other.

Dreamers have the capacity to see. Every great success was, at the beginning, impossible. Do not despise the days of small beginnings—David's kingdom became great but started small. Involve yourself with something larger than you are—God is there.

Mother Teresa had an encounter with God on September 10, 1946 that would define her vision and future. She would later describe it as "the call within the call." Teresa explained, "I was to leave the convent and help the poor while living among them. It was an order. To fail would have been to break the faith."[2] She obeyed God. As a result, her ministry—called *Missionaries of Charity*—was started in 1950 to care for the outcasts of Calcutta, India. It has ministered to thousands and continues to do so today. Her willingness to obey God's vision empowered her to become a mother to many and an extraordinary person.

Vision will empower and propel you into destiny. You will have faith to realize your dream when you can hear and see what God is offering you. Dreams come to dreamers who have positioned themselves in God's presence to see and hear what the Lord is offering. Have a listening ear and then follow Jesus wholeheartedly. God is inviting you to fulfill a destiny and to dream with him.

ACT ON YOUR DREAM
Faith and courage are essential to seeing your dreams fulfilled. David was courageous and valiant, and so was Jonathan. By

helping David, Jonathan was acting on his vision of a new kingdom and his role in it. Their dream and destiny were unfolding over time. They both, by God's design, were being prepared to reign in the new order.

Expect challenges to fulfilling your dream. David had seven years of wilderness training before he became king over the tribe of Judah. Your wilderness is preparing you for reigning with God. Quite often, it is in the crucible that God determines whether you are useable. Every leader and every dream is refined and tested; this is by God's design. Family, friends, finances, failure, and opposition will occur—be strong and of good courage. Embracing the process is required to fulfill dreams. Be persistent. Success is found in hard work and persistence. When asked about how many times he failed when creating the light bulb, Edison replied, "I didn't fail 1,000 times. The lightbulb was an invention with 1,000 steps."

David had another setback in Ziklag—his men talked about stoning him—but he encouraged himself in the Lord. Like David, many wonder how the setback occurred. Many ask God, "What about the dream? What about the promises?" You must be courageous in the face of adversity and take practical steps to realize your dreams. Pursue education, training, etc. Cultivate constructive discontent. Complacency never brings success— do not be satisfied with mediocrity. Escape from habit. Do not accept what is without considering what could be. Balance creativity with character.

EMBRACE CHANGE AND NEW SEASONS

Embrace new seasons and change with God's leading. Wisdom understands the new direction to take as the seasons change.

In Chronicles, we read of the sons of Issachar "who had understanding of the times, to know what Israel ought to do" (1 Chr. 12:32). They had wisdom and prophetic discernment regarding the times in which they lived. A listening heart and prophetic eyes will empower you to see new paths during cycles of change. Many miss their moment because they are unable to change with the season and dream. Sacrifice and hardship are often required to fulfill your purpose. Sadly, many stop at that point in their journey, for change is never easy and the challenges are many.

David went from being a shepherd boy to a warrior and captain overnight. It was a "suddenly," and the season changed. Jonathan recognized the shift and began—for several years—to move into the new season with David. Do you remember Jonathan's dream to serve alongside of David in the new kingdom? He loved David and could see what God was doing through him. He could even see his future alongside David. Yet Jonathan, however, had a strong tie to his family. When the moment came for him to shift into the new paradigm, he was unable to do so. Jonathan remained in the palace instead of following David into the wilderness. God was forming mighty men in the desert in preparation for a new dynasty. They were not impressive at first; in fact, they were a bunch of discouraged men that were drawn to David. God, on the other hand, was preparing the next generation of leaders and warriors. Palaces rarely produce great leaders—it takes the desert to refine them. Jonathan was unable to leave his family and the comfort of the palace. Time and tide wait for no man. Opportunities are veiled and require risk in order to achieve them.

At a time when Jonathan should have been alongside David and the other men, he went with his father and brothers to fight the Philistines on Mount Gilboa (1 Sam. 31:1-6). To a fault,

Jonathan was loyal to his family. He knew what God had revealed to him about David, but he lacked the courage needed to follow through with the dream and pursue new directions. Along with Saul and his brothers, Jonathan died in battle that day, and his dream died as well.

Jonathan could see what God was offering. He could see that change was coming, and he initially embraced the new dynasty. However, he was unable to let go of the past—the old order— to embrace the new move and season that God was unfolding. Jonathan's past and family ties prevented him from fulfilling his future. The cloud had moved, and at a crucial moment, Jonathan failed to make the needed adjustments to follow God. New paradigms require change and new strategies.

David lamented the death of both Saul and Jonathan, but especially his friend Jonathan (2 Sam. 1:17-27). I believe David mourned over both the loss of a close friend and over what could have been. Imagine for a moment the Davidic kingdom with Jonathan as King David's top aid and advisor. David and Jonathan could have been a powerful leadership team that impacted nations. David did go on to become a great king in Israel, seeing his dream coming to pass. Jonathan's dream ended tragically on a barren hillside. The tale of two dreams—one fulfilled, the other left desolate.

You will not fulfill your future if you are hindered by past failures, outdated thinking, or a lack of courage to move forward as Jesus leads you. New structures and new paradigms are needed in each generation in order to advance God's kingdom. In Acts 11, Barnabas took Paul to Antioch to minister to the believers, where they were first called Christians. In Acts 13 a shift occurred for the Church; a new apostolic-prophetic church was emerging in new territory where Jews and Gentiles were becoming "one new man" (Eph. 2:11-22). Jerusalem, while still important, was giving way to a new prototype of the Church.

Presently, the body of Christ is experiencing a new season. Significant shifts are occurring. Some are calling it an apostolic reformation, others a grace reformation. With the message of grace in their hearts, believers are once again functioning in the apostolic missional mandate of Jesus. New models of ministry are emerging to impact nations.

Yet the transition is not limited to the Church in this hour. Broad, sweeping geopolitical and economic changes are affecting our world. While these changes can be daunting, they offer great opportunities for business, education, medicine, entertainment, etc. The proliferation of modern technology and communication provides limitless possibilities for those who dare to dream. A global world is now just a click or two away—what impact will you make?

David transitioned into his future; he embraced the challenges and changes that came his way. Jonathan was unable to transition, and his dream and destiny died unfulfilled. Do not allow circumstances, time, others, or the enemy talk you out of the dreams and the promises God has given you.

KNOW THE TIMING

Let me state this again: time and tide wait for no man. The simple meaning of this ancient mariner's proverb is that no one can stop the progression of time and we should act on favorable opportunities right away. Even with today's modern technology, tides are significant for a sailor. The rising and falling of the sea affects water levels, and thus the ability for ships and boats to navigate the harbors and waterways safely. Any good sailor, or even a recreational boater, knows the hazards of a low tide in an ocean waterway, which could possibly strand you in port or, worse, run you aground onto the rocks or a sandbar. Fishermen also know that favorable tides create the best opportunity to catch fish; capitalizing on the right timing of the tidal flow increases the opportunity for a good harvest.

In the same way, farmers know the importance of seasons when planting their crops to ensure a good harvest. Farmers in the Midwest United States understand that frost or rains in the late spring can kill a newly planted field of corn or soybeans. Planting a field may seem like a trivial thing, but a modern-day farmer has thousands of dollars riding on the decision to plant the right crop at the right time. It takes wisdom, faith, and courage. If they plant too soon, it could be disastrous; conversely, if they wait too long, it could be equally detrimental as they need to be able to harvest before winter arrives. They have no margin to second-guess or doubt their ability. The farmer cannot let the nagging reminder of a failed harvest from the past hinder them from moving forward today.

The writer of Ecclesiastes states this truth: "For everything, there is a season, a time for every activity under heaven…A time to plant and a time to harvest" (Eccl. 3:1-2 NLT). Truly, knowing the type of season you are in and the proper timing to act on an opportunity that's before you is crucial for success. Have you noticed that some opportunities only come around once in this life? While, perhaps due to God's gracious design, some opportunities do present themselves again, the truth still remains that time keeps moving on and we must promptly capitalize on the opportunities that are presented to us—or they may be missed forever. David recognized God's timing and opportunity and realized dreams, Jonathan allowed the opportunity to pass and his dream died with him.

Since God knows the end from the beginning and the days fashioned for you even before you have lived a single one of them, isn't it reasonable to conclude that he already has your future in view, and you only need to learn how to cooperate with his divine plan?

THE SEED SHALL BE PROSPEROUS

In the beginning of 2009, the Lord spoke to me, "You are living in a Zechariah 8:12 moment." I quickly grabbed my Bible, looked up this verse, and read, "For the seed *shall be* prosperous, the vine shall give its fruit, the ground shall give her increase, and the heavens shall give their dew—I will cause the remnant of this people to possess all these."

As the Holy Spirit breathed on this passage, my faith soared for the financial provision needed for the new sanctuary I shared about earlier in the book. While on a mission trip to Brazil in the fall of 2005, God began to challenge me to "sow seed (finances) into India and watch for the sanctuary building I will give you." We have ministered in several nations over the years, but God was highlighting India at that time. We never give with a motivation of getting something back in return, but in this case, God made it clear that as we trusted him with giving to the poor in India, he would abundantly provide for us.

Normally, when a church needs to build a larger sanctuary, they form a building committee and start a building campaign. God had a different plan for us. Common sense would have said to put extra finances for a new building into savings rather than spend thousands on outreaches to India. However, we decided to take God at his word, and during 2006-2008, I made four trips to India, ministering to thousands in gospel meetings and leadership conferences. Hundreds came to Christ, many received healing, churches were strengthened, and leaders received training and equipping. Additionally, Passion Church sponsored the construction of a community center, which was also used for church meetings, in a village of Andrea Pradesh, India.

A PROMISE FULFILLED

When the Lord spoke to me that "the seed shall be prosperous," I knew by the Spirit that this word applied to the resources we gave to India during the previous years. I was convinced that God would perform the word he spoke to us and provide for the new sanctuary building. It was audacious, but God loves bold faith when he is leading—dreams happen in this realm.

God revealed his will during times of prayer and communion with him, and it then required faith and action on our part to be obedient to what he had revealed. Faith developed in my heart as I heard and understood what God was revealing (Rom. 10:17). God initially gave me and our church the faith to sow seed into India. Then, God gave me faith to believe that the finances previously given to India would produce a harvest—our new church sanctuary. It was an unusual building program to say the least!

When the Lord spoke to my heart that "you are living in a Zechariah 8:12 moment," faith rose within me that the "seed would be prosperous." I knew it was an accomplished fact in the heavenly realm. Both of the words from God imparted a grace for faith and the confidence to pray, knowing that it was the will of the Father. As I came to the Father in prayer concerning the provision for our new building, I simply reminded him of his promises: "Father, you said that if we sowed seed into India, then you would provide for us a new sanctuary building. Father I thank you that we are living in a Zechariah 8:12 moment, and that our seed shall be prosperous and yield heaven's increase. Father, I thank you for your provision and for this new building—Amen!" The result: the new church sanctuary was constructed during a seemingly impossible economic season. As I shared earlier, God unfolded a financial miracle for us during one of the worst financial periods in our nation since World War II. In the kingdom of God, there is neither lack nor recession. Jesus is enough, always!

When we live by kingdom economics, we receive from kingdom resources. To do so, we had to think outside of the box and get creative to finance the project. Yes, God provided miraculously for the building—giving soared and finances came in. However, the bulk of the money came from selling church bonds—this was a different paradigm for us, but God was in it. Had we doubted God's leading, we would have missed the moment and opportunity. Always be ready to change and adapt in order to see your dream fulfilled.

I want to encourage you to wait upon the Lord, commune with him, and simply ask him to provide revelation and faith for that which you are praying (Jer. 33:3). Once received, agree with God, declare heaven's decrees, and watch what he does here on earth. He loves to bring our dreams to pass. God may do it in unusual ways, so be ready to change and adapt as required.

Seize Your Day!

You are daily becoming more like Jesus as you walk with him, and you are changing from glory to glory in his presence. You are an imitator of God—you reflect your Father. You are living from your union with Christ and his nature. You are identified with him, not with your past. At the core of your new nature is love for Jesus and for people. God is love, and those who love others are of God. Love propels you to care for those around you and represent God. Love is the foundation for lasting dreams.

God created you to be an extraordinary person—in both character and achievement. Settling for mediocrity was never God's plan for you. You are not merely heading to a destiny fulfilled; your journey is unfolding into destiny. Don't settle for comfort or ease—choose to follow God wholeheartedly. From a place of love, serve Jesus as a faithful disciple. He has extraordinary things for you. Dare to seize your day!

END NOTES

Chapter One

1. Merriam-Webster Dictionary, http://www.merriam-webster.com/dictionary/extraordinary, retrieved July 3, 2015.

2. Movie, *Dead Poets Society*, http://www.independent.co.uk/arts-entertainment/films/news/robin-williams-best-dead-poets-society-quotes-carpe-hear-it-carpe-carpe-diem-seize-the-day-boys-9663800.html and http://www.imdb.com/title/tt0097165/quotes, retrieved June 29, 2015.

Chapter Two

1. American Literature: Mark Twain, http://americanliterature.com/author/mark-twain/bio-books-stories, retrieved July 3, 2015.

2. Mark Twain: Tom Sawyer Whitewashing the Fence, http://www.pbs.org/marktwain/learnmore/writings_tom.html, retrieved July 3, 2015.

3. Merriam-Webster Dictionary, http://www.merriam-webster.com/dictionary/courage, retrieved July 13, 2015.

Chapter Three

1. Chris Byrley, "Healing," ed. Douglas Mangum et al., *Lexham Theological Wordbook*, Lexham Bible Reference Series (Bellingham, WA: Lexham Press, 2014).

2. Henry George Liddell et al., *A Greek-English Lexicon* (Oxford: Clarendon Press, 1996), 1429.

3. Dallas Willard, *The Great Omission* (New York, NY: HarperCollins Publishers, 2006), 61.

4. Gerhard Kittel, Geoffrey W. Bromiley, and Gerhard Friedrich, eds., *Theological Dictionary of the New Testament* (Grand Rapids, MI: Eerdmans, 1964–), 447.

5. Johannes P. Louw and Eugene Albert Nida, *Greek-English Lexicon of the New Testament: Based on Semantic Domains* (New York: United Bible Societies, 1996), 513.

6. George Peck, *Throne Life: The Highest Christian Life*, (Boston, MA: The Watchword Publishing Co., 1888), 41-42.

7. Johannes P. Louw and Eugene Albert Nida, *Greek-English Lexicon of the New Testament: Based on Semantic Domains* (New York: United Bible Societies, 1996), 154.

Chapter Four

1. Miles Custis, "Fear," ed. Douglas Mangum et al., *Lexham Theological Wordbook*, Lexham Bible Reference Series (Bellingham, WA: Lexham Press, 2014).

2. Johannes P. Louw and Eugene Albert Nida, *Greek-English Lexicon of the New Testament: Based on Semantic Domains* (New York: United Bible Societies, 1996), 598.

Chapter Five

1. Robert L. Thomas, *New American Standard Hebrew-Aramaic and Greek Dictionaries: Updated Edition* (Anaheim: Foundation Publications, Inc., 1998).

2.   Gerhard Kittel, Gerhard Friedrich, and Geoffrey William Bromiley, *Theological Dictionary of the New Testament* (Grand Rapids, MI: W.B. Eerdmans, 1985), 783.

3.   Ibid., 449.

Chapter Six

1.   Gerhard Kittel, Gerhard Friedrich and Geoffrey William Bromiley, *Theological Dictionary of the New Testament* (Grand Rapids, MI: W.B. Eerdmans, 1985), 1037.

2.   Roger L. Hahn, *Matthew: A Commentary for Bible Students* (Indianapolis, IN: Wesleyan Publishing House, 2007), 227

3.   Joshua G. Mathews, "Blessing," ed. Douglas Mangum et al., *Lexham Theological Wordbook*, Lexham Bible Reference Series (Bellingham, WA: Lexham Press, 2014).

4.   Loring T. Swaim, Arthritis, *Medicine and Spiritual Law: The Power Beyond Science* (Philadelphia, PA: Chilton Co., 1962).

Chapter Seven

1.   Caroline Leaf, *Who Switched Off My Brain?* (Southlake, TX: Switch on Your Brain International LLC, 2007), 4.

2.   Ibid., 49.

3.   http://www.huffingtonpost.com/don-joseph-goewey-/85-of-what-we-worry-about_b_8028368.html, retrieved June 8, 2016. http://www1.cbn.com/700club/jentezen-franklin-fear-fighters, retrieved June 8, 2016.

4. Oswald Chambers, *His Utmost for His Highest*, https://www.facebook.com/MyUtmostForHisHighest/posts/10153520958863423, retrieved March 23, 2016.

5. Johannes P. Louw and Eugene Albert Nida, *Greek-English Lexicon of the New Testament: Based on Semantic Domains* (New York: United Bible Societies, 1996), 314.

6. Ibid., 312.

7. Gerhard Kittel, Gerhard Friedrich, and Geoffrey William Bromiley, *Theological Dictionary of the New Testament* (Grand Rapids, MI: W.B. Eerdmans, 1985), 987.

8. Johannes P. Louw and Eugene Albert Nida, *Greek-English Lexicon of the New Testament: Based on Semantic Domains* (New York: United Bible Societies, 1996), 798.

9. https://twitter.com/tozeraw/status/488031079672983552?lang=en

Chapter Eight

10. Mary Healy, *The Gospel of Mark* (Grand Rapids, MI: Baker Academic, 2008), 128.

11. Smith Wigglesworth, *Ever Increasing Faith* (Springfield, MO: Gospel Publishing House, 1971), 81.

12. Charles S. Price, *The Real Faith for Healing* (Gainesville, FL: Bridge-Logos Publishers, 1997), 9.

13. Friedrich Hauck, "Περισσεύω, Ὑπερπερισσεύω, Περισσός, Ὑπερεκπερισσοῦ, Ὑπερεκπερισσῶς, Περισσεία, Περίσσευμα," ed. Gerhard Kittel, Geoffrey W. Bromiley, and Gerhard Friedrich, *Theological Dictionary of the New Testament* (Grand Rapids, MI: Eerdmans, 1964–), 60.

Chapter Nine

1. https://www.wholesomewords.org/missions/biotaylor2.html, retrieved November 11, 2017.

2. Wilhelm Michaelis, "Κράτος (θεοκρατία), Κρατέω, Κραταιός, Κραταιόω, Κοσμοκράτωρ, Παντοκράτωρ," ed. Gerhard Kittel, Geoffrey W. Bromiley, and Gerhard Friedrich, *Theological Dictionary of the New Testament* (Grand Rapids, MI: Eerdmans, 1964–), 908.

3. Gerhard Kittel, Gerhard Friedrich, and Geoffrey William Bromiley, *Theological Dictionary of the New Testament* (Grand Rapids, MI: W.B. Eerdmans, 1985), 254.

4. Mark Batterson, *The Circle Maker* (Grand Rapids, MI: Zondervan, 2011), 87.

5. https://www.brainyquote.com/quotes/quotes/c/calvin-cool414555.html, retrieved November 3, 2016.

6. Johannes P. Louw and Eugene Albert Nida, *Greek-English Lexicon of the New Testament: Based on Semantic Domains* (New York: United Bible Societies, 1996), 627.

7. Ibid., 375.

Chapter Ten

1. James Swanson, *Dictionary of Biblical Languages with Semantic Domains: Greek (New Testament)* (Oak Harbor: Logos Research Systems, Inc., 1997).

2. Sadhu Sundar Singh, *At the Master's Feet*

3. Merriam-Webster Dictionary, http://www.merriam-webster.com/dictionary/trust, retrieved November 4, 2016.

4. James Strong, *A Concise Dictionary of the Words in the Greek Testament and The Hebrew Bible* (Bellingham, WA: Logos Bible Software, 2009), 102.

5. Ernst Jenni and Claus Westermann, *Theological Lexicon of the Old Testament* (Peabody, MA: Hendrickson Publishers, 1997), 610.

Chapter Eleven

1. James Strong, *A Concise Dictionary of the Words in the Greek Testament and The Hebrew Bible* (Bellingham, WA: Logos Bible Software, 2009), 38.

Chapter Twelve

1. Mother Teresa, *Helping the Poor* (Brookfield, CT: The Millbrook Press Inc., 1991), 20.

ACKNOWLEDGEMENTS

—m—

I AM GRATEFUL FOR THE many who have helped me grow in Christ and aided me in my journey—thank you. I am indebted to Dr. Randy Clark, Dr. Tom Jones, Dr. Tom Litteer and many other friends and associates of Global Awakening—you have helped shape my ethos—thank you. I am especially thankful for the Passion Church family and leaders who have believed in and supported me as their pastor the past 16 years. I want to thank Glenn Wristen, Jason Anderson, Karen Pierson, Danielle Baethge, Samuel Anderson, Hannah Goswick, and my wife Carolyn for being such a great church staff. You have helped shoulder the load enabling me to teach, speak, and write—thank you. I am also grateful for Julia Vinton and Danielle Baethge for your edits of the initial manuscript, and Dr. Azure Maset for your comprehensive editing of the final manuscript. Thanks to Trevor Crosby and the team at Magmod for the cover portrait photo. Thanks to Jenny Chandler and the team at Elite Editing for the cover design and book layout. Thank you to the many who prayed for me as I wrote this book—Jane Quijada, Karen Pierson, Diana Bramlett, Elise Arnold, and Terri Travers in particular. A special thank you to my wife Carolyn for your prayers, love, and support through this project—you enabled me to dream and write this book into existence.

ABOUT THE AUTHOR

—⬥—

In 2002, Dr. Bob and Carolyn Sawvelle established Passion Church in Tucson, Arizona. Prior to coming to Tucson, they served as missionaries in Haiti and as youth and missions pastors in Florida. Over the years, they have made numerous short-term ministry outreaches to Belize, Brazil, Guatemala, Haiti, India, Israel, Mexico, Mozambique, Romania, Tanzania, Ukraine and Venezuela.

In 1994, while on a stateside trip from Haiti, they were powerfully touched by the Holy Spirit in meetings at Catch the Fire Toronto, and then again in 1995 during meetings with Dr. Randy Clark in Melbourne, Florida. Since that time, they have desired nothing less than to be filled with God's presence and to allow his love and power to flow through them to change and heal the lives of others. Bob has a heart for the poor and hurting, and he believes that God is wanting his people to carry God's love and power beyond the four walls of the church buildings to those in need. Bob has a passion to teach and equip the body of Christ to operate in the fullness of the gospel of the kingdom.

Bob and Carolyn have been trained in healing ministry through Global Awakening Ministries and Catch the Fire Ministries. Additionally, they have received training in prophetic ministry from Christian International Ministries and Global Awakening

Ministries. They both are ordained ministers. Bob has a M.Th. and D.Min. degrees.

Bob has published two books on healing, *A Case for Healing Today* and *Receive Your Miracle Now*. Bob is a course facilitator with Global Awakening's online Christian Healing and Prophetic Certification (CHCP and CPCP) programs. He is also a doctoral mentor at United Theological Seminary (UTS), working with leaders who are earning their doctorate in ministry degrees with the Randy Clark Scholars group at UTS. Bob also teaches Master's level courses at the Global Awakening Theological Seminary (GATS).

More written and video teachings from Bob can be found on his website bobsawvelle.com, passiontucson.org, and on his YouTube and Facebook pages.

CPSIA information can be obtained
at www.ICGtesting.com
Printed in the USA
LVHW020936180620
658260LV00008B/1186